Memories
of
Slough

Part of the
Memories
series

*The Publishers would like to thank the following companies for supporting
the production of this book*

East Berkshire College
GD Evans Limited
Flexello Limited
Kidde Graviner Limited
Harris & Cartwright Solicitors
Haymill Saab
ICI Paints
Kopex International Limited
Mars Confectionery
National Starch & Chemical Limited
New Zipper Company
Observatory Shopping Centre
Ragus Sugars plc
Sara Lee Household & Bodycare Limited
SEI Macro Group
Slough Borough Council
Geo Streamer Limited
Tunes Engineering Service Limited
Versatex Limited
W N Thomas & Sons Limited
Wyeth

First published in Great Britain by True North Books Limited
Units 3 - 5 Heathfield Industrial Park
Elland West Yorkshire
HX5 9AE
Tel. 01422 377977
© Copyright: True North Books Limited 1999

ISBN 1 900463 29 6

Text, design and origination by True North Books Limited
Printed and bound by The Amadeus Press Limited

Memories are made of this

Memories. We all have them; some good, some bad, but our memories of the town we grew up in are usually tucked away in a very special place in our minds. The best are usually connected with our childhood and youth, when we longed to be grown up and paid no attention to adults who told us to enjoy being young, as these were the best years of our lives. We look back now and realise that they were right.

So many memories - perhaps of the war and rationing, perhaps of parades, celebrations and royal visits. And so many changes; one-way traffic systems and pedestrianisation. New trends in shopping that led to the very first self-serve stores being opened.

Through the bad times and the good, however, Slough not only survived but prospered. We have only to look at the town as it is today to see what progress has been realised and what achievements have been made over the last 50 years. Slough has a history to be proud of - but more importantly, a great future to look forward to, into the new millennium and beyond.

Contents

Around the town centre

In the 1930s, the talkies were all the rage in the cinema. For long years people had gone to the flicks and seen just that, flickering black and white pictures. The scenes were captioned, as there was no soundtrack on the film. Down in the pit below the screen, a pianist would play mood music to help us get into the right frame of mind for what we saw. The famous Violet Carson, as Ena Sharples - one of the original cast of TV's 'Coronation Street', began her career playing love themes as Rudolph Valentino smouldered before our eyes. On the very right is the Palace Cinema where locals came to wonder at those early movies that brought the voices of the stars to us. Some could not make the transition from the silent film era because their speaking voices were not up to it. We will never know whether Valentino's career would have blossomed, because he died in 1926. One pair who did cross over was Douglas Fairbanks and Mary Pickford. He was a swashbuckling heartthrob and she the 'American sweetheart'. They were married in 1920, though divorced 15 years later. The Palace could not have had a less glamorous background. It had been EA Purser's butcher and fishmonger shop. The cinema opened in 1921. Locals flocked to watch Pickford in 'Pollyanna' and Fairbanks in 'The Three Musketeers'. Any snippets of a newsreel of the day would have given a glimpse of Jack Dempsey, the Manassa Mauler, defeating the handsome Georges Carpentier to retain his world heavyweight boxing title. The Palace was renamed The Century in 1949 and closed in 1957. Two years later it became Waitrose.

Left: At the Windsor Road crossroads, pictured about 1930, Foster Brothers' store was trading from the place formerly occupied by the Slough tailoring Company. So well known did it become that some locals referred to the area as Fosters' corner, rather than the more usual Crown corner. The garage at Fullbrook House, across from Fosters', was normally a busy establishment. Perhaps the photograph was taken on a Sunday. Fullbrook and Company Motor Works, to give its full title, was built on the site of the Black Boy public house and opened for business in 1925. The 'horseless carriages' were starting to make their mark amongst the more affluent. Traders began to do away with the horse and cart as a means of moving goods around, though you could see a number of these on the road up to the outbreak of World War I. Their first trucks were often war surplus vehicles from the Great War. The inn was knocked down in 1910, but one legend about its clientele lives on. A notorious highwayman used to drink here. Claude Duval could be seen spending the ill-gotten gains of his deeds on the Bath Road. Cries of 'Stand and deliver' would bring him sovereigns, watches and trinkets to finance his toping in the Black Boy. However, a life of crime was not a basis for a long and healthy life. Claude was captured and had his neck stretched at Tyburn in 1670.
It was around this crossroads that the first hamlet of homes appeared in medieval times.

Below: Slough was one of the few towns to have escaped the worst excesses of unemployment in the early 1930s. The Trading Estate had become the life blood of the district. Whilst other areas struggled to make ends meet, leading to protests like the 1936 Jarrow march on London, Slough prospered. The Ministry of Labour's Employment Exchange was just that. Elsewhere, it might be an exchange for the unemployed, but here jobs were to be had. The central section of High Street, from Boot's, on the left, down to Hilton's on the corner of Church Street, was well blessed with signs of that prosperity. Shoppers were spending their money and new furniture was being bought for the homes that were springing up on the new estates on all sides of the town. The motor cars pictured are not ordinary runabouts. Sleek limousines, with those 'Eliot Ness of the Untouchables' style of running boards and side mounted spare wheels, drove smartly along. They would have cost a pretty penny or two. Timothy White's and Greville's photographic studios can be seen on the left. Across the road, Maxwell, Boynton's, Rodman's and Bacon's have been replaced by the new shopping centre. The clock was a landmark on the Leopold Institute and Public Hall. The Duchess of Albany opened it. She was the widow of Prince Leopold, Duke of Albany. He was the youngest son of Queen Victoria. Photographs of the building made charming Christmas cards or picture postcards.

Above: At Crown corner, the imposing Imperial buildings were erected in 1931. The view of the western end of High Street, where it becomes Bath Road, dates from just after the opening of the newly modelled home for the Fosters' Clothing Company. Before then it had been known as Foster Brother' Clothing Company. On this side of the road locals now come to town to change their books or consult reference material in Slough Library. Opposite, Fullbrook House was a busy garage, recognised by the two major motoring organisations, the RAC and AA. In 1999, control of this latter body was taken over by Centrica, which has a large office on Windsor Road, behind where Fullbrook House was sited. In the early 1930s there

Slough began to expand in the 30s thanks to the earlier birth of the Trading Estate

was little thought of business development in the country. These were the days of the depression and companies were going to the wall, in many cases. Slough, though, was out of step with the rest of the land. It had started to expand. Mainly thanks to the birth of the Trading Estate the decade before, there was work to be had. Housing estates were built to provide homes for the workers in the factories. Stoke Poges Lane estate had already been completed. New houses at Meadfield, Manor Park, Upton Lea, Chalvey, Cippenham and Baylis Court soon followed. The workers produced sewing machines, electric irons and vacuum cleaners. As their homes had electricity, they bought what they produced and helped make housework a lighter task.

Right: It must have been a daunting matter to make a phone call from the box on Crown Corner. Standing in the middle of the road, with traffic passing in front and behind, meant you needed eyes in the back of your head. Many a nervous caller cut short a conversation when the threat of the Austins or Schweppes wagons racing by became too much to bear. Even in the early 1930s, this was one of the traffic black spots in town. The photograph was taken, looking north along William Street, from the place locals referred to as 'the Bottleneck'. Before the building of the bypass, traffic ground to a halt here on a regular basis. People travelling from Windsor, in the south, or Stoke Poges, to the north, met the London to Bath road at this very spot. To make matters worse, there is a distinct kink in the road here. This made passage through even slower as allowance had to made by reducing speed, so that the offset crossroads could be negotiated safely. It is thought that the odd path that the road traced was due to an old elm tree that once stood here. First mention of it in records is made in 1604. The tree was still there as late on as 1830. By that time, the long distance stagecoaches, as well as the local traffic that passed through the Bottleneck, had established the shape of the road.

Below: The Methodist Central Hall was demolished in 1966; but, around 1932, it still stood out as a landmark on the corner of the Grove. The building that had been occupied by the National Westminster Bank was renamed and opened in an official ceremony by the Duchess of York. Born Elizabeth Bowes-Lyon, she had little idea what the future held for her. By the end of 1936 she would be the Queen, as consort to George VI, following the abdication of her brother-in-law, Edward VIII. From the date of her daughter's coronation as Elizabeth II, she became known to the entire nation as the 'Queen Mum'. Pictured from Grove Parade, looking east, is the front of the nursery of Charles Turner. He took over Brown's nursery in 1848. 'The answer lies in the soil' was one of the catchphrases used on Kenneth Horne's famous radio shows of the 1960s. It fitted the nursery that Turner developed. That most famous of apples, Cox's Orange Pippin, had first been grown in Colnbrook in 1830. He developed its commercial cultivation in 1850. Following a royal visit from Queen Victoria, in 1878, it became Turner's Royal Nurseries. He lived in a fine house here, its grounds stretching as far north as Wellington Street and east to Wexham Road. Charles Turner continued to develop his green-fingered skills. He introduced several new strains of roses, including the Crimson Rambler. He deservedly earned the nickname 'King of the rose growers'.

Ashwell's was one of a number of outfitters that traded on High Street in the early 1930s. Clothing is really only needed to provide warmth and protection. However, it became another way of enhancing sex appeal and displaying wealth and social class. In the Western world, changes in fashion have often been dictated by the wealthy. They could afford new fabrics and designs. These then trickled down to the lower social classes through the ready to wear shops. Styles would have been copied and cheaper materials used. By the time we got into our new set of togs, the fashion world was onto its next phase. The rich and chic could not be seen in yesterday's clothes or those worn by the common person in the street. Britain had a part to play in the history of fashion development. As a

major player in the textile industry, it pioneered the
three piece lounge suit for men. As Eastern dress
has been more traditional, Asian peoples brought
their own distinctive styles into the country in large
numbers in the mid to late 20th century. There has
been some influence of these cultures in British
dress, of late. No chance of any such effect upon the
chap by the lamppost in the picture. He was firmly

working class. His large flat cap was the very symbol
of the working man for much of the 20th century.
His wife's dark and sombre practical clothing would
stand out against the bright saris and shalwar-kamiz
that decorate the High Street in modern times.
Next to Ashwell's was Walsden's chemist shop.
Across the way, above the Green Line bus, was where
the Gas and Coke Company had its premises.

Above: HD Bowyer was one member of a family that had business and civil links with Slough for over a century. His building and contracting firm is busy, this day in the early 1930s, on Windsor Road. He did not have far to travel to work there. Harry Bowyer's company had its headquarters on Mackenzie Street, near where the Reindeer Inn used to stand. The site of the premises is now under the Queensmere Shopping Centre. Harry had inherited the business from his father, John Bowyer. It was in 1866 that John and his brother, Thomas, set up their building firm on Park Street, close to where Upton Hospital now stands. Thomas Bowyer's son, Edward, was very active in local politics. He became Mayor of Slough in 1938. The Bowyer building company, having celebrated its centenary in 1966, went bust four years later. The view is one of the Crown Hotel in the distance, with the Rising Sun closer to hand. Feminists in the modern era would have a field day with the idea that a pub could reserve a saloon bar just for its male customers, but that is what the Rising Sun did. Any poor female who ventured across that threshold in the 30s would have received short shrift. By the end of the 20th century, some of these parts of Windsor Road were looking a little dowdy, although this was countered by the smart offices occupied by Centrica, the law courts and council offices further to the south.

Right: This aerial view was taken in 1933. The importance of High Street is clear as it dominates the scene, running diagonally across the photo-graph. To the right and north of the street, St Ethelbert's Church stands out on its spot in between Mackenzie Street and William Street. The kink at 'the bottleneck', where Windsor Road and William street meet, shows one of the reasons that traffic used to build up here, as the road was not a straight run through. It always was a busy road, but especially in the 20th century when Londoners could get by car to the spa city and posh tea rooms of Bath. The A4 hummed with traffic. Before public ownership, privately owned companies charged tolls to use roads that had first started to see a volume of traffic in the 17th and 18th centuries. Such roads were called turnpikes, after the revolving spiked frames that could be used as barriers. Bath Road was turnpiked in 1727. Coaches had begun to make the journey to the spa waters in 1716. The ease with which London could be reached, along what was to become the A4 and with the coming of rail travel in the mid 1800s, meant that Slough was recognised as one of the first of the capital's commuter towns. It came a long way in a short time. In 1841, there were just 1,189 people living here. However, this figure only referred to Slough centre and Upton. By 1861 the number had risen to 4,600. It doubled before the end of the century and grew to over 11,000 in 1901.

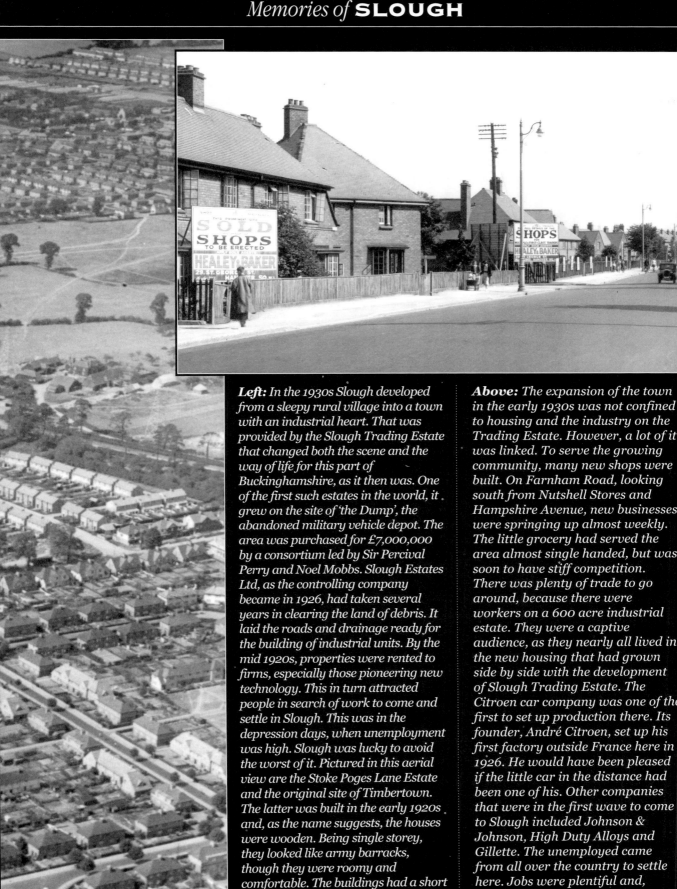

Left: In the 1930s Slough developed from a sleepy rural village into a town with an industrial heart. That was provided by the Slough Trading Estate that changed both the scene and the way of life for this part of Buckinghamshire, as it then was. One of the first such estates in the world, it grew on the site of 'the Dump', the abandoned military vehicle depot. The area was purchased for £7,000,000 by a consortium led by Sir Percival Perry and Noel Mobbs. Slough Estates Ltd, as the controlling company became in 1926, had taken several years in clearing the land of debris. It laid the roads and drainage ready for the building of industrial units. By the mid 1920s, properties were rented to firms, especially those pioneering new technology. This in turn attracted people in search of work to come and settle in Slough. This was in the depression days, when unemployment was high. Slough was lucky to avoid the worst of it. Pictured in this aerial view are the Stoke Poges Lane Estate and the original site of Timbertown. The latter was built in the early 1920s and, as the name suggests, the houses were wooden. Being single storey, they looked like army barracks, though they were roomy and comfortable. The buildings had a short life span and were demolished in the 1930s. Herschel Grammar School stands there today. The Horlicks factory, on the left, produced the famous malted milk drink that did away with night-time starvation and gave us all a good night's sleep.

Above: The expansion of the town in the early 1930s was not confined to housing and the industry on the Trading Estate. However, a lot of it was linked. To serve the growing community, many new shops were built. On Farnham Road, looking south from Nutshell Stores and Hampshire Avenue, new businesses were springing up almost weekly. The little grocery had served the area almost single handed, but was soon to have stiff competition. There was plenty of trade to go around, because there were workers on a 600 acre industrial estate. They were a captive audience, as they nearly all lived in the new housing that had grown side by side with the development of Slough Trading Estate. The Citroen car company was one of the first to set up production there. Its founder, André Citroen, set up his first factory outside France here in 1926. He would have been pleased if the little car in the distance had been one of his. Other companies that were in the first wave to come to Slough included Johnson & Johnson, High Duty Alloys and Gillette. The unemployed came from all over the country to settle here. Jobs were plentiful and, although the wages were not good, they were enough to encourage the new shopkeepers that cash registers would soon be jingling. This part of Farnham Road still had a large number of shops at the end of the 20th century.

Above: The central part of High Street has not changed in one respect. It is still the busiest part of town. Traffic is no longer allowed and the shops might have changed. Perring's Bedding, on the right, has long gone, but the activity remains just as intense. On this stormy morning, around 1960, we are looking west from the junction with Chandos Street, that is off to the right of the Post Office. This street used to connect High Street with Wellington Street. On this site you can now find an entrance to the Queensmere Shopping Centre. This entrance to the centre is called Chandos Mall in memory of the street it replaced. It is good to see that the developers kept some links with the past by retaining some of the old names within their plans. It was on Chandos Street that James Elliman had his first factory, where he manufactured his famous embrocation. The Post Office stood on this corner from 1893 until its demolition in 1972 to make way for the shopping centre. Slough had got its first main post office in 1841. Maria Luff, who was the landlady of the White Hart, became the town's first Postmaster. Sir Rowland Hill had proposed changes to the country's postal system in a series of reports in the mid 1830s. Eventually, he was able to launch the penny post in 1840. With the increase in business this brought, Mrs Luff moved to larger premises at 1 Buckingham Place. That building was demolished in the 1990s, but the Post Office moved on from there at various times in the 19th century, before settling at this spot on Chandos Street.

Above right: On the left, Church Street now marks the end of the western end of the pedestrianised section of High Street. The photograph was taken from opposite Park Place buildings that date from the 1840s. They were shops with two floors of accommodation above. Next door to the Hilton

boot and shoe shop was Neville and Griffin. As the road curves across William street and Windsor Road, the Grapes stands looking back at you up the road. It had been giving that view from its impressive frontage since 1830 when it was first licensed. Then it was called The Traveller's Friend. This name reminds us of the important position held by Slough on the London to Bath road. It was a busy coaching route for both passengers and the mail. From as early as the mid 1600s, carriages would rattle along past here. The journey to Bath from the capital took several days and travellers as well as horses needed a watering hole. The first mail coaches were privately owned businesses. John Palmer of Bath ran the first service in 1788. However, it caused annoyance to Slough residents. Although the coach came through here on a daily basis, it dropped off the mail in Maidenhead! Locals then had to make a special journey to collect it. A compromise was reached in 1812 when letters were left in Colnbrook and, for the cost of a penny, delivered by a messenger to Slough. The town was not then large enough to support its own post office.

It is a good time to be alive in Slough. The old exists alongside the new. Exhaust fumes of lorries and cars can live comfortably with the horse droppings of a bygone age. Seen from the Floral Arms, a pub since 1872, looking towards where the Queensmere Centre is now situated on the right, the motor cars look a little like those we have seen on the newsreels from Chicago. Sitting in the cinema, we gazed in amazement as gangsters jumped onto running boards and machine-gunned everyone in sight. Nothing like that would ever trouble Slough High Street. Thanks to the Trading Estate, there was plenty of work to be had and money to be spent in the shops. Ladies could get their hair done professionally at Keymilla. How

we sweated for ages, our heads stuck under those machines and tightly wound curlers straining our hair at the roots. But it was worth it. With a bit of luck, there would be a copy of that new magazine, Picture Post, for us to flick through. Eventually, out we would pop, looking like Vivienne Leigh or one of the Andrews Sisters. Well, we could dream; but, not for much longer. There were rumblings from the other side of the Channel. The Germans were about to annexe Czechoslovakia and Austria. Spain was in the throes of civil war and Mussolini had invaded Abyssinia. It was to be a good time for only a short while more. Keymilla and Bridger, next door, had once been H Bryant's photographic studios.

Looking west along the High Street, the London Drapery Stores sit across the road from Isaacs, on the right. The awnings that have been drawn down will protect the shoppers from the downpour that is about to come as the skies seem leaden with the rain that they will drop on the unfortunate housewife trying to fill her shopping basket on this day in the mid 50s.

The awnings have another purpose. They advertise the name of the store and keep the sunlight from fading the upholstery and furniture on display in Isaacs' shop window. Soon pac-a-macs and plastic rainhoods will join the umbrellas as the Slough shoppers struggle to keep dry. The High Street had a very different feel and sound to it in those days. By the

end of the 20th century, it had become a cosmopolitan place to be. You could walk along its pedestrianised way and listen to the voices of a dozen different languages. You could mix with many other races and admire the dress of various cultures that have made the town their home in recent years. In that first decade after the war, you might hear the occasional Polish voice. A number of displaced Poles or those who had fought with us in the forces settled here. But, in later years, you were just as likely to hear Gujerati or Hindi being spoken as you were English. Sometimes, you might hear that strange sort of tongue the Americans speak, as they puzzle out how to pronounce our town's name. 'Say, buddy, is this Sluff I am in?'

Right: High Street in the 1950s was a bustling scene. It still is today, as the shopping centre of the town. Then, it was a through road, not given over to the pedestrianised area, as we know it now. Lorries, vans and cars made their way along it and there were lines of cars parked along the way as shoppers went about their business, not worrying about overstaying their time at the pay and display on the Grove. Looking east from the Methodist Central Hall to Wexham Road, Times Furnishing is to the left and the Bucks Music Stores further along near Boltowns. It was a time when rationing was becoming a thing of the past and we were beginning to come out of the austere days of that early postwar period. In that short time there had been changes to the way we lived. A Labour government had swept to power in 1945. Nationalisation, education reforms and the birth of the NHS had all taken place. Perhaps we blamed Mr Attlee for not making us wealthy overnight. We had won the war, but there was so much to do in rebuilding our country and our lives. Money was tight and food and other goods still in short supply. Winning the war had not meant immediate prosperity. So, in 1951, we returned to Mr Churchill as our leader. Perhaps he could bring some more goodies to our shops on the High Street.

Below: The British Home Stores came to Slough in 1937 when the shop took over the building that had been Lidstone's. Looking east along the High Street from the cinema, the home of the Methodist Central Hall can clearly be seen. The National Westminster Bank had stood on this site until 1932. The Central Hall was occupied until 1966. It was at this time that many of the older buildings disappeared. Redevelopment was in the air. Wexham Park Hospital was built in 1965 and the nearby M4 motorway attracted much new traffic. In the 1950s, High Street was the main road through the town. It was finding it difficult to cope with the increase in traffic as more affluent times came. Many of us owned cars for the first time and traffic jams came along as well. The dual carriageway that would bypass Slough was begun in 1967. The bikes parked at the kerb on the right show some people's ways of defeating the crawl by car. As the 20th century drew to a close, the government was turning back the clock by encouraging councils to build cycle lanes and more no go areas for cars. The pedestrianised part of High Street now has special bike parks where the cycles can be racked and locked away safely until the cyclist has finished his business in town. Pedestrians have to take care when the odd pushbike comes nipping past. Better that, though, than being mown down by a motor car.

The headscarf became acceptable in the 1950s - even more so when the Queen was caught on camera in hers!

Walking across from Church Street, this woman today would be more likely to head off to her right. It is now the pedestrianised area of the town. The Queensmere has replaced the buildings on the left of the photograph. The woman in the picture shows attitudes that were common in 1950. A lady went to town with her head covered. It was very racy to go around bareheaded. Those who wanted to dress up could put on a hat, but for everyday use, the headscarf was the mode of dress that was followed. As well as covering the head, it might have hidden a set of curlers as she was crimping her hair ready for a night out. This was not in the best of taste, for most of us. The headscarf became even more acceptable later in the 1950s. It was given royal approval when the Queen was caught on camera wearing hers. This was not a case of being snapped unawares. The headscarf was part of her normal casual attire. If it was good enough for her, then the rest of us could follow suit. Milward's and Hilton's', in the left and right of the photo, were two shops that rivalled each other for trade in the selling of shoes. The clock marks the site of the Leopold Institute and Public Hall. It was opened on 6 December 1877 and demolished in 1972.

Above: The woman crossing central High Street, at the corner of Church Street, cannot be impressed with the lack of care or consideration shown by the cyclist. The Belisha beacons, flashing out an orange warning of their existence, do not seem to have any effect on this roadhog. Perhaps we are about to witness an example of pedal rage, if an argument ensues. It is doubtful; the pedestrian looks to be too nice a lady to lower herself. Let us hope that the cyclist signs up for the Slough Safety scheme that was to come along in 1955. She could certainly do with some coaching in cycle proficiency and road safety. Leslie Hore-Belisha had introduced his distinctive beacons when he was Minister of Transport in the mid 1930s. By 1950, around the time of this scene, he had become Baron Devonport. Behind our pedestrian, the young mum is also keeping a wary eye out for other traffic. The pram she is pushing was a wonderful vehicle. At times it could double as a coal carrier, but as a receptacle for shopping, packed around junior, it kept one hand free to hold tightly on to the other nipper, making sure he did not wander. It was a useful bed for putting down the littlest one for his afternoon nap. Right now, baby seems to be taking it all in. There might be some new playthings to be got from Suter's store to put round his Silver Cross. Just let them try to put coal in here!

Right: This part of the town is now very different from this 1952 scene. It is now a marooned part of the High street, cut off from the main shopping areas by the busy road that runs across the picture. As Windsor Road/William Street it provides one of the main access roads towards the M4 and the A4 bypass. As can be seen from the road sign, the main road ran straight across that junction in the middle of the 20th century. The corner, where Franks stood in part of the Prudential Buildings, is Crown corner. Beyond there, High Street shopping starts in earnest. A photograph taken today would show Slough Library in place of the buildings on the left. You cannot get a pint of Courage ale there now, but, when the White Hart was in business, it was well known for the quality of its beers. It had first gained fame as a coaching inn. Built in the 1630s, it could claim to be one of those places acting as the second stage on the road out from London. As there were a number of coach companies operating on the London to Bath route, there were also several different stops on the way that were able to make this claim. The other inns around Slough that also acted as stage posts included the Crown, the George at Colnbrook and the Windmill at Salt Hill. Coach suspension was poor and tired and weary travellers were glad to ease their aching limbs with a tankard or two before bouncing off down the road again.

During the 1950s petrol rationing came and went - doing nothing to slow down the rate of car ownership

This part of the town has been known as Crown corner for more years than anyone can remember. The reason is easy to understand. On the right of the picture is the pub sign for the old Crown Hotel. This view of High Street is looking east towards the Grove and Grove Parade. The Queensmere shopping centre now dominates the upper left hand side of the street. You can still drive along this part of the High Street, but even in the 1950s it was becoming a slow journey. High Street had started to be a place to avoid if you wanted to get to Uxbridge, Maidenhead, Windsor or some other neighbouring town. That was easier said than done as the bypass would be another decade away. During the 50s petrol rationing had come and gone. First as a wartime measure, other restrictions came with the 1956 Suez crisis. The Egyptian president, Colonel Nasser, seized control of the Suez Canal. He said that the imperialist powers could 'choke on their own fury'. The inconveniences did little to slow the rate of car ownership in Britain. Lines of traffic often clogged High Street, leaving motorists plenty of opportunity to gaze at the winkle pickers or sling backs in the shoe shop windows. For others there was the chance to look at the Dior inspired 'A' line dresses or wide petticoated frocks favoured by the younger generation.

Below: The residents of Timbertown, built around the Farnham Road, complained bitterly that there were no leisure facilities for them in the area. Complaints were made to their employers on the Trading Estate. Locals also put pressure on their local councillors to do something about it. Politicians in the 1930s were just as aware as now of the power of the ballot box. Faced with such a swell of feeling, the council was happy to support the initiative that several of the estate's companies took on board. In 1936, the Slough Social Fund was set up. The following year, Slough Social Centre, built at a cost of £45,000, was opened to the public. It had just the wide range of activities on offer that people wanted. So varied were they, that people from all walks of life were attracted there. As well as games and pastimes, it had rooms for exhibitions and wedding celebrations. It was one of the first of its type in the country. King George VI and Queen Elizabeth (later to be known as the Queen Mum) visited in late 1937. They had a game of darts and no-one was surprised that our monarch lost to his wife. That was typical of the character who became the best loved of the

Royal family in the second half of the century. Seen here, looking south down Farnham Road, across Buckingham Avenue, the Centre became Slough Community Centre in 1957. A new building, just called 'The Centre', replaced it when it was demolished in 1997.

Bottom: Tarmac and buildings cover the ground on which Slough was built. At first, there were boggy marshlands around here. The town name means 'wetland'. It has had other unofficial descriptions. Perhaps one of the best remembered, and worst deserved, is that given to it by a former poet laureate, John Betjeman. 'Come friendly bombs and fall on Slough; it isn't fit for humans now.' Those unkind words are as out of place now as they were this day in the 1950s. The southeast view of High Street shows many of the shops that had been well established here. Hepworth's, Littlewoods, Scotch Wool, Timpson's and Timothy White's were just a few of the varied retail outlets that attracted the Saturday morning shopper. Some of the older buildings would have been constructed using local

materials. Slough was famous for its brickfields. Bricks had been made in the area since 1442. Eton College was built with 2,500,000 bricks supplied by Slough. The Slough crest has two brickaxes on it, maintaining the town's link with its heritage. The industry was working at its greatest capacity in the late 19th century. A team or 'stool' of six men could average a production of 5,000 per day. Several of the local housing estates in Slough and Langley were built in the lowlying ground where the brick earth had been removed. The last hand made bricks were manufactured in 1939. The shops and stores in this picture would prefer to thank the 'brickies' for their existence than Mr Betjeman for his sarcasm.

Bottom: There is many a smart young man about town who went to the 'window to watch' to get his best bib and tucker for that night out on the tiles. John Collier, around 1960, was a tailoring name to be found on most of the country's main shopping streets and parades. Young men did not go out for the evening in casual gear. That was denounced as being sloppy. Even the pop groups of the day went on stage in smart suits. Woe betide you if your mother had to say, 'You're not going out looking like that, are you?' John Collier had the range of sports jackets and suits that would kit you out nicely for that evening at the dance hall when Joe Loss or some similar band would mix the latest music with the good old standbys. You had probably bought a Rael-Brook poplin shirt from Collier's, as well. That was the non-iron shirt that could dance on the washing line. Further to the west was the Waitrose store, one of the first supermarket style of shops to come here. One item being advertised that has little changed is Heinz ketchup. According to its slogan, 'adds that fine taste', it had been doing just that for nearly a century. There is no reason to think that it won't continue, for what is a fried breakfast without a dollop of tomato sauce to go with it?

Right: Around 1960 prosperity had returned to Britain. It was a period of near full employment and wage packets were fatter than they had been for some time. There were new clients for the shopkeepers as teenagers became a buying force in their own right. The start of the swinging 60s, that were to swing even more wildly before they were finished, had been ushered in by a famous speech from our prime minister, Harold Macmillan. On his way to victory in the 1959 election, he told us 'We

had never had it so good'. Supermac's words rang true on High Street. The line of private cars, parked outside Waitrose and John Collier's, stretch along eastwards towards the distinctive dome of the Methodist Central Hall. Shiny chrome and American style tail fins for rear wings marked out some of the cars of the day. The Velox, the Consul and the Victor all stood spanking new on our driveways or streets as we became a nation of car owners. No longer was the motor car a luxury. It was now an essential. The bus was a decidedly poor man's mode of transport when you had your own car to take you to the shops or off to work. Even if we could not manage the full amount for our new chariot, there was always HP. So much down and the rest over 36 months became the norm. Sadly, no-one told us that those lovely tail fins were inclined to hold the rainwater and became rust traps before we had finished paying off the arrears.

At leisure

It had to be a bright sunny day to get so many people out of doors. No heated pools for these bathers in the 1930s. Despite the sunny weather, the water temperature was only warm enough to tempt the most daring of swimmers to do much more than dip in a toe from time to time. Montem Pool was a popular gathering place. Situated in the Salt Hill Playing Fields, there were ice creams to be had and games to be played on the grass. The girls in their swimsuits might have wanted to pretend to be Esther Williams, the movie star who spent so much time in the water. However, Esther would have been swimming in the warmth and not shivering after being exposed to the dubious benefits of the open-air pool. Mum insisted that her daughter wore a little swimming cap. As well as keeping the hair dry, it was also more proper for a young lady to keep her head covered when in public. The bikini was a garment that was still on the horizon. How would granny have reacted to the thong? Many dads were still wearing one piece costumes. This part of Slough owes its name to traditions of a bygone age. Montem refers to a medieval mound or motte. The mound of earth was a well protected defence point, surrounded by a ditch. In the 16th century, boys from Eton College were initiated in a ceremony whereby they were sprinkled with salt. This was supposed to represent wit. In later years, a custom developed that the boys could come here to collect money from passers by, in exchange for a pinch of salt.

Boys' clubs were a popular way of occupying idle hands and using up excess energy. While the lads were enjoying their time in Farnham Road Social Centre, later to be known as the Community Centre, they could not get up to mischief. These clubs were meant to be character building. They offered a number of activities that these scallywags might not have had the chance to try out. As well as sports like boxing, soccer and table tennis, they had the chance to have a go at drama productions, woodworking activities and occasional debates. Some boys' clubs had their own bands and day trips out were always popular. The aim of such clubs was stated to be 'a boy is a person who is going to carry on what you have started'. It was a sound ideal. Help the boy to start out on the straight and narrow and he will continue to follow that path for himself. Adult coaches were happy to give of their time and come to the club and train the youngsters. Perhaps amongst their ranks a future soccer star like Bobby Charlton or Gordon Banks could be found. In this 1938 scene of the boxing ring, the left jab and left hook are being promoted. Maybe the former British heavyweight champion, Henry Cooper, learned to use his famous 'Henry's Hammer' of a left hand in this way. Boxing was seen as a noble art and was taught in many schools before the powers that be decided it was too dangerous.

Below: Having spent a pleasant afternoon at the Social Centre, locals could happily walk a few hundred yards up the Farnham Road to the junction with Essex Avenue and Furnival Avenue. There they found the Ambassador Cinema. In 1952, they would have been able to spend hours of enjoyment in the darkened auditorium. There was a continuous showing of the programme. Many times people came in part way through a film and waited until it was shown again. With the well known phrase of 'This is where I came in' they would be off back home once more. Those with little else to do might even watch the whole lot over and over. In the 50s you got value for money. There would be two films to see, though the 'B' movie was usually dire, starring Ronald Reagan as it might have done. The squawking cockerel of Pathé News introduced the newsreel that brought us the only moving pictures of events we would be likely to see. Television was in few homes. We might also have seen the adverts from Pearl and Dean, the latest antics of Tom and Jerry and the trailers for next week's blockbuster. A drink on a stick and a lad's shoulder to rest your head on made it a night to remember. Come Saturday afternoon and we could get rid of our kid brother to the matinée and let him enjoy the cliffhanging episodes of Flash Gordon and the crazy world of the Three Stooges. That's all, folks!

Bottom: Dancing is an art form. Whether it is the headbanger, the breakdancer or the flamenco expert, each has its special moves. It is unlikely that one sort understands or appreciates the other. What does it matter, as long as you are having fun? Slough has held a special place in its heart for the more formal style of dance. Names such as Ken Bateman and Blanche Ingle bring back memories of the ballroom dance being performed with a style none of us could hope to match. The slow, slow, quick-quick, slow of our foxtrot was light years away from the way they performed it. Formation dancing, when teams would compete against others, has been popular for half a century or more. TV's 'Come Dancing' was one of BBC's top programmes. The men were handsome in their dinner suits and the wonderfully sequinned gowns of their partners dazzled. The Slough Amateur Modern Formation Team practised hard in the Community Centre on Farnham Road. All that hard work paid off. In the photograph the team is taking part in the ninth annual Festival of Reunion, sponsored by the holiday camp king, Billy Butlin. The Slough team got all the way to the final for the open Amateur Modern Formation Trophy. The contest was held in the finest arena possible, the Albert Hall. When the team walked off with the prize, shirt buttons nearly popped as chests swelled with pride. In the late 1990s, it was decided that ballroom dancing could become an Olympic event. Take your partners, please, for the gold medal.

Bottom: Upton Court playing fields have seen some strange sights, but were they prepared for these intrepid go-carters in 1962? The Mayor, Noel Eschele, was with Frank Warwick, Cllr Alan Simpson and the Parks' Superintendent, Leslie Scrase. We do not know whether they actually raced these, but, if they did, the chairman of the road safety committee, who was Mr Warwick, might have had something to say. The least these ageing boy racers should have been wearing was a crash helmet. There was a serious side behind the fun and games of this posed picture. Back in April 1955 the Minister of Transport, J Boyd-Carpenter had opened the experimental Slough Safety Town scheme. The town was chosen as an average example of the growing problems facing Britain's roads as the volume of traffic increased at this time. There were quite a few ideas spawned during the two years it operated in Slough. Not all were successful, or popular. Even so, a number of the initiatives were adopted and are still in use today. Speed traps and police wielding radar guns appeared for the first time. Yellow lines were painted to restrict parking and the High Street got traffic light controlled crossings. The dreaded traffic wardens came on the scene and, elsewhere parking meters popped up on the pavements. A better reception was given to the cycling proficiency and road safety classes aimed at protecting the children. There were motor cycling courses and cars, for a while, got a free health check. Let us hope these four chaps were paid up members of the Tufty club.

Right: This was a skilled operation. Four trained technicians, led by Mr H Clayton, were working in partnership in a hot and sweaty room. High above the popcorn eaters in the tuppenny seats, the projectionists of the Ambassador Cinema fed the cans of film into their machines. Doing their best to ensure that there was no obvious gap between reels, they balanced sights and sounds to bring us the best entertainment that the late 1930s had to offer. All we could see from our seats was the beam of light, specks of dust floating around in the beam that shone onto the silver screen in front of us. Sometimes, when things went wrong, there would be a whirr and a clang as a film snapped and all we saw was a grey outline. Whilst the men got busy upstairs, cutting and splicing, we joined in the ritual of stamping our feet on the floor, sometimes to the chorus of 'Why are we waiting?' Before too long, they had fixed the problem and, to a cheer, the house lights dimmed again and we were ready to carry on watching the latest Hollywood epic. That year we would have been wowed by the acting of the magnificent Greta Garbo. Along with Fredric March, she entranced audiences in 'Anna Karenina'. At home, all talk was of the Rochdale throstle, Gracie Fields. Having entertained us with songs like 'Sally' and 'The biggest aspidistra in the world', she had signed a two year contract with Associated Talking Pictures. 'Our Gracie' was to make three films at the Ealing studios for the unheard sum of £150,000.

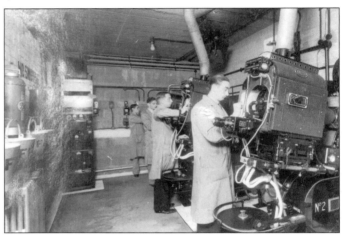

This picture could have been captioned 'Heads you lose', because everyone seems to have missed the ball completely. Airbrush the ball away and you have a perfect ready made competition - spot the ball. Those sort of competitions were very popular in the 1960s, from when this action shot dates. Punters put their little crosses on places where they thought the ball might be and off their entries and postal orders would go to the newspaper organising what was supposed to be a game of skill. When the full answer picture, complete with ball, was published, was it ever anywhere near where we thought it was? Try it out. Cover the ball and doesn't it look as if the player on the right has headed it well to the

Slough Town Football Club was founded in 1890 and moved to Wexham Park in 1974

right? No wonder we lost. This match was played at Dolphin Stadium, the home of Slough Town. Dave Kemp knocked in the last ever goal scored there. He was later to manage the side. The club that was founded in 1890 moved to Wexham Park in 1974. The Park was a ground devoted to football. There were no other distractions or competition from the cycle and dog tracks that had plagued the previous administration. At that time, the club was in the Isthmian League, playing in front of crowds averaging around 400. By the 1995/96 season, Slough Town had reached the top level of non League football, playing in the Vauxhall Conference. No continued fairy tale success for Slough Town, though. Millennium celebrations took place with the club down in the Ryman Premier League.

Events & occasions

Fire is fascinating. One of the first warnings a mother gives to her child is not to crawl near the fire. The bright light attracts like a magnet. Even as we get older, the sight of flames flickering in a camp fire, or roaring through a building, brings people to crowd together. As children, we used to chase the fire engine on our bikes. Whenever we heard the clanging bells and saw the shiny red monster racing down the street, off we went in hot pursuit. Things don't change when we reach adulthood. Just look at the knot of people that has gathered to gaze open mouthed at the Old Crown Hotel. As smoke billows from the roof, shop assistants join with passers-by to gawp at the sight. Fortunately, there was to be

only minor damage. Thank goodness for the brave boys of the fire service. Hoses were swiftly attached to hydrants and out came the ladders to help direct water onto the flames from above. However, there must be a method in fighting the fire effectively. Even in 1929, the Slough brigade knew that, which is the reason for the discussion in front of the building. The fire had to be contained and other buildings and people protected. Ventilation was needed to allow hot gases or toxic fumes to escape and firemen to gain access. Then they could go to work. Organised fire brigades can trace their history back to Roman times. Emperor Augustus set up the first official firefighting force in 7 BC.

Bottom: Balloons and flags, ribbons and flowers all decorate the carnival float in 1933. The Co-op employees stand stiffly to attention as they pose for their picture outside Slough Station. Very soon they will take their place on the cart and others will sit aloft Goddard's vehicle as they set off to parade through the town before finishing off with fun and games on the Bowyer Playing Fields. The carnival celebrations were popular with young and old alike. The games and sports that were held at the end of the parade attracted some 1,000 children in 1905. As the town grew in size and the carnival in popularity, the number of entrants to the kiddies' races and fancy dress competitions had risen to 3,000 by 1938 - a figure to rival the Olympics!

Slough and District Co-operative Society went from strength to strength during the first half of the 20th century. It was the main sponsor of these carnivals. In a way, they helped us forget the horrid history that had caused people to band together to form such societies. In the 1840s, the 'hungry 40s', people were dependent on the manufacturing companies. Wages were cut and shopkeepers mixed sand with oatmeal and plaster of paris with flour to bump up profits. Food and goods had to be bought, at inflated prices, from the 'badger' shops owned by the bosses. In 1891, a group of railway workers set up a shop to help the starving families of the brickfield workers who had been locked out of work in an industrial dispute. Slough Co-op was alive.

Right: You could get your daily pinta from Mr Bunce, the friendly CWS milkman. Handcarts were pulled around the street in the first home deliveries, but the horse drawn carts soon replaced these. The little electrically powered floats were for a later age. 'You can save money by buying from the CWS' was a simple slogan. Mr Bunce's son, astride the crates, looks happy to reinforce the slogan as he waits to join the 1933 carnival parade. To order milk, the householder left a token on top of an empty bottle. The first dairy opened in Chalvey. Milk came in tankers, having been collected from the farms in the large, clanking churns that were hauled up onto carts to be brought in for pasteurising and bottling. The milk was put into the dairy cold store. The rounds' foreman counted out the bottles when the milkmen came in to collect them. Their empties were checked and put into a washer, ready for the process to start all over again. On one occasion, the washer broke down. It was out of action for three days. If the men thought that meant a nice little holiday, they were sadly mistaken. All 50,000 bottles had to be washed by hand!

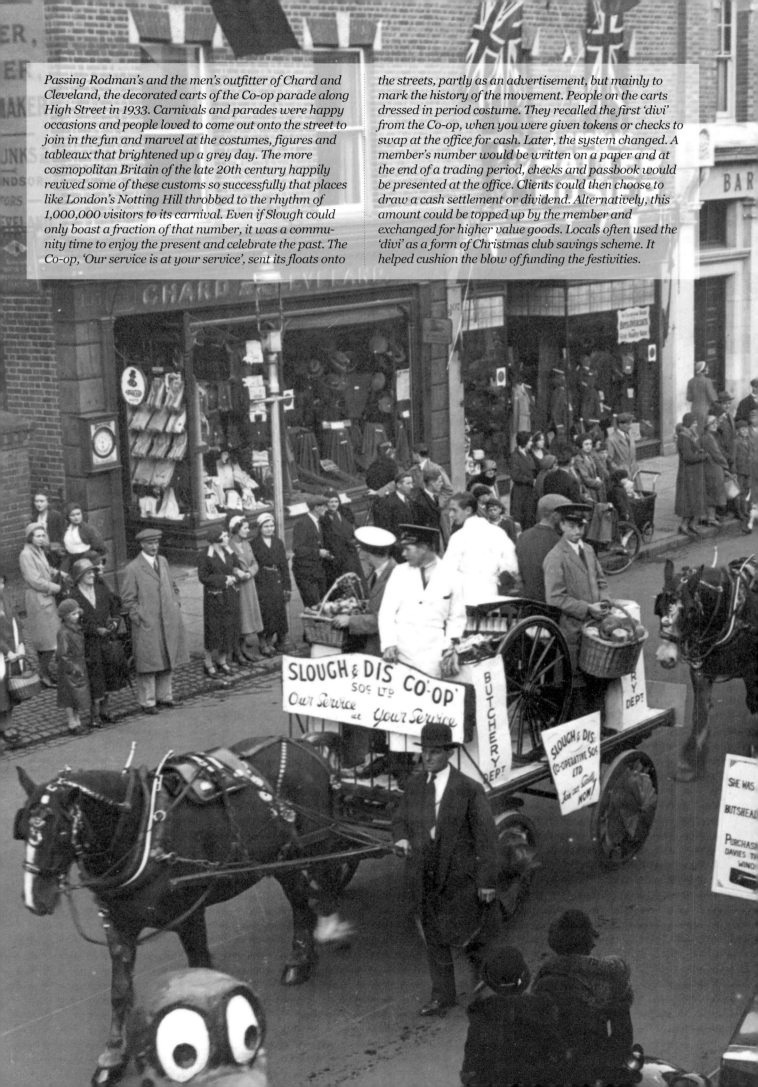

Passing Rodman's and the men's outfitter of Chard and Cleveland, the decorated carts of the Co-op parade along High Street in 1933. Carnivals and parades were happy occasions and people loved to come out onto the street to join in the fun and marvel at the costumes, figures and tableaux that brightened up a grey day. The more cosmopolitan Britain of the late 20th century happily revived some of these customs so successfully that places like London's Notting Hill throbbed to the rhythm of 1,000,000 visitors to its carnival. Even if Slough could only boast a fraction of that number, it was a community time to enjoy the present and celebrate the past. The Co-op, 'Our service is at your service', sent its floats onto the streets, partly as an advertisement, but mainly to mark the history of the movement. People on the carts dressed in period costume. They recalled the first 'divi' from the Co-op, when you were given tokens or checks to swap at the office for cash. Later, the system changed. A member's number would be written on a paper and at the end of a trading period, checks and passbook would be presented at the office. Clients could then choose to draw a cash settlement or dividend. Alternatively, this amount could be topped up by the member and exchanged for higher value goods. Locals often used the 'divi' as a form of Christmas club savings scheme. It helped cushion the blow of funding the festivities.

The flags were waving and the lines of bunting gaily danced on the lampposts and telegraph poles. Old and young turned out for the four days of celebrations that marked the arrival of Slough as borough, in its own right. Never mind if there was trouble in Czechoslovakia. Mr Chamberlain, our prime minister, would deal with Herr Hitler and make sure that the Czechs were safe and that there would be peace in our time. There were things at home to celebrate. Last month, Len Hutton had helped England thrash the Aussies by beating Bradman's Test record. Len scored 364 and his record would stand for 20 years until a West Indian youngster, Garfield Sobers, would beat it. In the meantime, these were days to remember how our town had developed and the

place it holds in English history. The telegraph poles had become commonplace, but Slough had led the way in pioneering its use in sending important messages. The first piece of telegraph line was brought here in 1843. Slough Telegraph Cottage was situated near the North Star Inn and people came to wonder at it on special open days. The town telegraph hit the headlines in 1845 when John Tawell murdered his mistress, Sarah Hart, in Salt Hill. He escaped on the train to Paddington, but the police were notified when they were wired ahead, using the new marvel of the times. Tawell was arrested at his lodgings. He was the first murderer to be caught by the use of the telegraph. Those poles in the photo carried more than just bunting.

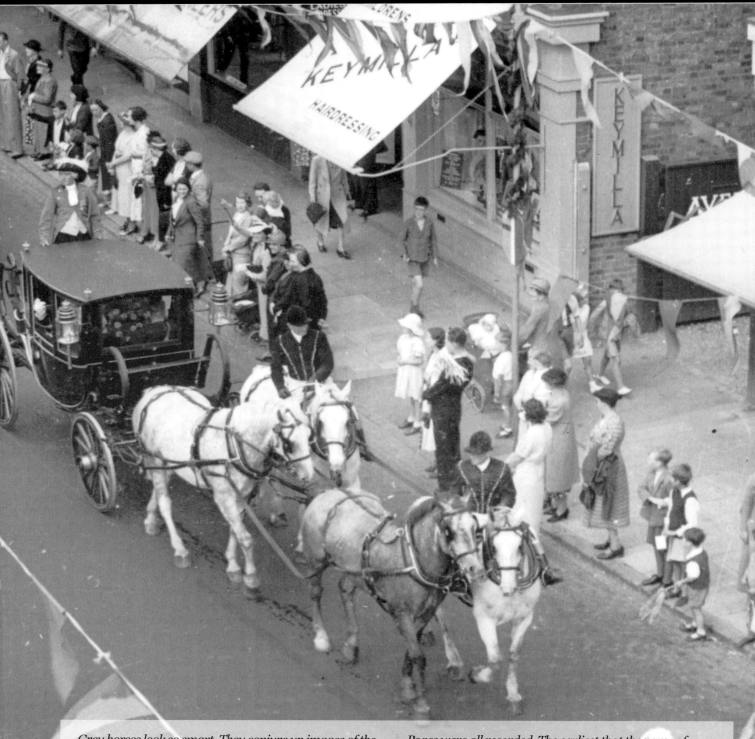

Grey horses look so smart. They conjure up images of the dashing white chargers described in books where the action was based in the centuries of long ago. On a day when Slough people looked forward to the future of the town as a borough, it was good to look back on the traditions of the past. The dancing plumes of the outriders, on their way to Lascelles Playing Fields, added a dignity to Charter Day that the residents of Slough appreciated. They left the hairdryers and crimping sessions in Keymilla and came onto the streets to witness a parade, the like of which they had seldom seen before. When William the Conqueror had the Domesday Book compiled, villages in the Slough area were mentioned. Upton, Farnham, Ditton and Stoke Poges were all recorded. The earliest that the name of Slough was to be seen occurred in a taxation document of 1196. Then it was called Slo. The town really only grew from being a village in the 19th and 20th centuries. It was not until 1863 that Slough became a district of local government, with a local Board of Health. It was afforded the title of civil parish in 1894 and, later that year, became recognised as an urban district, administered by the UDC. Boundary changes, at the start of the 20th century, saw Slough include Stoke Road, Chalvey, Salt Hill and part of Langley in its responsibilities. By the time the charter was signed, further boundary changes expanded Slough's net at the start of the 1930s.

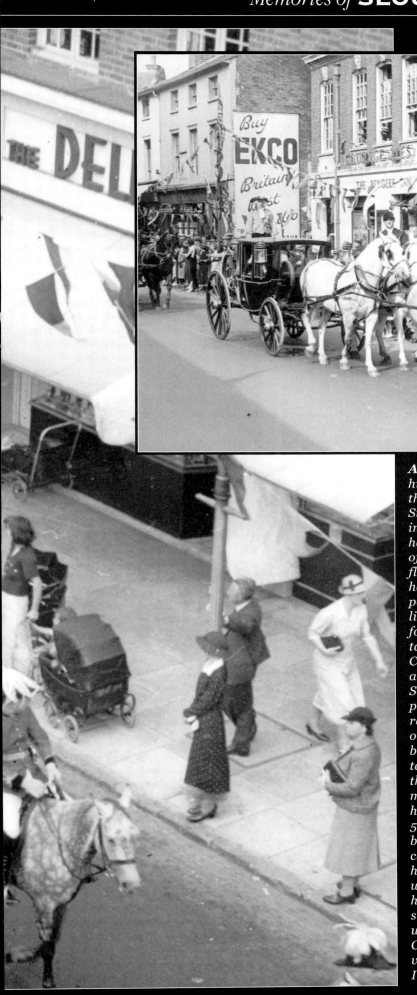

Above: *The Ekco radios being advertised
hummed with the news of the great day. As
the ceremonial coaches bowled along High
Street, townspeople emerged onto the streets
in thousands. Passing by Burton's, the horses
had to be carefully watched in case the noise
of the crowd and the movement of waving
flags startled them. They wore blinkers to
help cut down the distraction from the
pavements and the bunting above. The
liveried footman stood proudly on the
footplate of the coach that carried the digni-
taries to the celebrations to recognise
Charter Day. The town gained its charter as
a borough in 1938. For four days in
September there were ceremonial functions,
parades, speeches, parties and fairs to
recognise Slough's coming of age. The
origins of Slough are lost in the mists of time,
but life must have begun on the Taplow
terrace created by the shifting movement of
the Thames. It was around 7,000 BC when
man first set foot in the area. Early peoples
hunted and fished, for it was not until about
5,000 BC that metal working skills were
brought in by new settlers. The pomp and
ceremony of Charter Day recognised the
history and traditions of the past. At the time
when Christ was alive, Saxons came to live
here. Some of the local place names still
show links with those times. Upton was the
upper village and Langley the long clearing.
Cippenham was quite simply, Cippa's
village. Chalvey shows the link with farming.
Its name means the island of calves.*

During the period of rejoicing that Slough observed in Charter Week, the mayor and his colleagues on the council made official visits all over town. Hospitals, church groups and schools were all included. The children at Tonman Mosley School were reminded of how the town had grown. In medieval times, it was Upton cum Chalvey, with a handful of small settlements making up the population. They were told of the manor house at Upton Court, that had been just one of many on the estates in Cippenham, Chalvey and Upton. History lessons included the development of the council, and how it used to levy a rate of 1s (5p) in the £ and distribute the proceeds to the poor in early Victorian times. Children realised how quickly things had changed. Only 40 years before, the council offices were in rooms over Headington's shop on the High Street. Now the town could boast its own mayor. The pupils learned about the great astronomer Herschel and his discovery of the existence of the planet Uranus. They were reminded of Observatory House on Windsor Road, where Herschel had built his giant telescope. The house stood until the 1960s. These little girls would have listened carefully to all this. Dressed in their little frocks, with neatly ribboned hair, they belonged to an age when children listened to and learnt from the adults who spoke to them. White ankle socks and sensible shoes were the appropriate wear for the primary school student in 1938, not like the fashion parade of the modern miss.

Below: The carnival marked the final day of the four day celebrations that surrounded the granting of the borough charter. Fun and games were the best ways to remember such an important time. All very well to have the official functions and necessary to have the pageantry, but to mark the end of the period with something for the children seemed just right. After all, they were the ones who, as adults, would have to take the borough forward into the second half of the 20th century. The schoolchildren's sports were no hit and miss affair. In keeping with the dignity of the day, the races were carefully organised and willing volunteers checked the entrants to the start lines. Running shorts, official numbers on the athletics vests and pumps ready to set off running made sure that everyone treated the day seriously. There was even a proper running track marked out in lanes. The children loved it, though some parents always took these sorts of things too seriously. Isn't it embarrassing to see a grown man screaming at his young son to go quicker or run harder? Perhaps he gets some sort of reflected glory if his lad does well. Though, heaven help the poor soul if he comes last. At least, in 1938, there was no problem with these athletes being on performance enhancing drugs or having to take a dope test if they won a certificate! However, rumour has it that Molly McMahon was disqualified from the egg and spoon race for illegal use of the thumb.

Three cheers for Mr Mayor. Here he is in all his finery and the young 'uns in Upton Court Park were letting him know their delight in being part of the Charter celebrations. Edward T Bowyer held the unique position of being the Charter Mayor. The son of a builder and cousin to Harry Bowyer of HD Bowyer's building firm, Edward was an auctioneer and estate agent. His interest in public service saw him elected as a councillor in 1912. By 1922 he had become a county councillor. He continued to support his town right up to his death in 1944. Those children around him will be drawing pensions by now, but they will still remember that September day in 1938 when Slough became a borough and the town was allowed its first mayor. As senior citizens today they will tell of the fun that they had, watching the parades and rushing around on the dodgems at the fair. There were now 50,000 people living in Slough. The youngsters were too little to appreciate that Slough's development and progress had now been recognised by an official Charter of Incorporation. The Lord Lieutenant of Buckinghamshire presented it to the Charter Mayor. It was only under local government reorganisation in 1974 that Slough became part of Berkshire. Further changes came in the 1990s, when Slough became a unitary authority under yet another local government reshuffle.

Above: Even in so called times of peace, there was still national service. Men were called up to spend two years in military training to prepare for the defence of our country, should the clouds of war gather again. There were also various auxiliary and voluntary groups who met on a part time basis. These often provided a breeding ground for those who went on to become regulars in the armed forces. One such group was the Air Training Corps (ATC). A Slough division met at St Paul's Church. Here the church parade of the ATC can be seen marching along Stoke Road. It is 7 March 1954 and Warrant Officer Quayle leads his section of young men and lads. Bugles blew and the drums were beaten to signal the start of the march. Parishioners followed behind to demonstrate their membership and faith. Parades like this were a common sight on our streets in the 1950s and 1960s. The Whit walks were the main occasions to show off our solidarity. They were days when we dressed up in our new clothes and walked behind the brass band before rushing off to see our uncles and aunts, who we hoped would dole out a few shillings for our moneyboxes. However, this day in 1954 was many other things. It was a reminder of the marching boots of the armies in the war. It was a warning about the unrest in other parts of the world. That same day, Mau Mau terrorists in Kenya were being captured and the Germans were demanding the return of private property from the Americans.

The future would see marching groups in Ireland still causing violence nearly half a century later.

Below: This was just one of many coach outings organised for ex-servicemen in the late 1940s. The coach belonging to E Sargeant & Son would take them off for the day to talk over old times and look forward to a brighter future. There would also be a chance to reflect on the fate of those who were not as fortunate and had fallen on some foreign field, in defence of King and country. Their names are recorded in the Slough Book of Remembrance, 'lest we forget'. The friendships forged in battle by these men were ones that would last a lifetime. When you have fought shoulder to shoulder with a comrade, relying on him for your own survival, you do not easily dismiss that bond in peacetime. The British Legion was established earlier in the century as both a place where ex-servicemen could meet and as an organisation that could help look after their interests. Politicians made so many promises about a world fit for heroes and remembering the sacrifices our brave boys had made. But, when it came down to it, the bowler hatted brigades in the corridors of power fudged the issue. As ever, the common man and woman were left to sort out the future at a personal level. Never mind, they did not expect much else. Talk on the excursion would not bother with politics. There was Bradman's last Ashes tour to discuss and the rude things in that American Kinsey's report to chuckle over.

Above: In the late 1950s the Community Centre on Farnham Road buzzed with the sound of happy voices on dance night. When the band came on stage to play, most of us took to the floor. This was before the days of the twist and the shake, when couples began to dance apart from one another. On dance night, then, a lad took you in his arms and whisked you round the floor to the music of the quickstep. Later there would be time for a good old smooch in the last waltz. Live bands provided the music. Just putting on records was youth club stuff. This was the night out of the week and the musicians were there to entertain us. While the others danced, some made their way to the front of the stage to get a glimpse of the professionals who had come to town this evening. The dark haired woman at the front of the crowd has a look of Jackie Kennedy, who married the future American president in 1953. She is as fascinated as anyone with the showmanship of the band. Musicians had to be versatile. As well as playing the old standards, they had to keep up with the times and work in some of the modern pop tunes into their repertoire. One of the best of that era was the Joe Loss Orchestra. With lead singer Ross McManus, father of 80s and 90s pop star Elvis Costello, it was popular for over 30 years.

Above right: Princess Elizabeth had only another year to go before she would be the Queen. Sadly, her father, George VI, was already in the first stages of lung cancer when she came to preside at the official opening of Slough College. By now, she was representing him at many state and official occasions, including the Trooping of the Colour. She was preparing for a change to her life that would mean less time for her two children. They were still little. Charles was not yet three and Anne had only been born the previous August. It would not be until 1960 that she would add to her family.

In 1951 there were many proud governors and civic officials standing in line to greet her. Higher education had been something that was largely reserved for the privileged or super intelligent. After the second world war there was a drive to widen the intake and encourage youngsters from all walks of life to broaden and extend their education. There were other paths for the working class than just following the one that led to the factory floor. For 40 years the College provided teenagers with that chance to better themselves. In April 1991, the College merged with Ealing College and Queen Charlotte's College of Health Studies. The new Thames Valley University was born. In 1996, Tony Blair MP, who became prime minister the following year, opened a multimedia learning resource centre on the Slough campus. Important as he was, the occasion lacked the sense of tradition present in the Royal visit of 1951.

Wartime

This poor little tot is not the subject of some appalling experiment. Nor is she about to be blasted off into space. The strange looking contraption was something designed to save her life. It was a gas mask. In World War I, there were horror stories about the use of mustard and chlorine gas that crippled and killed so many soldiers. In the Spanish Civil War that began in 1936 there had been accusations that the use of such weapons, although outlawed, had been revived. Britain was taking no chances when war broke out again in 1939. Air Raid Precaution (ARP) had been set up as part of the nation's civil defence in the years leading up to the outbreak of hostilities. It had become obvious that

German rearmament and the aggressive attitude of Italian and Spanish fascists might result in war, once more. The Women's Voluntary Service (WVS) was set up in 1938 to support the work of the ARP. Before long, church halls and schoolrooms would be filled with anxious mothers, keen to find out about the best first aid treatments and protection for their families from gas attacks that could be launched from a bomber aeroplane. The toddler may look ridiculous in her helmet, but the breathing tube could just as easily provide her with life as the umbilical cord had when she was born. Mothers take no chances when it comes to defending their young. Appearances were no matter; preservation was.

Never mind the token male to the right, it is to these women that we will be looking to keep the home fires burning, the wheels of industry turning and the fields producing. He will be off to the front, but the immediate future of our homeland depends so much on the efforts of the women and girls we can see in front of us. It is 1939 and the spade in the background reminds us to dig for victory. These women and girls will have to dig deep into their own resources in the years to come. Pictured near Wexham Road Bridge, they are workers at McMichael's. It was a company that manufactured radios. During the war, the communications industry developed as companies, like this one, met the government demand for improved technology. It was vital to keep in touch with ships at sea, planes in the air and generals at the front. Leslie McMichael was an amateur radio buff. He started a radio club in 1913 that went on to be the Wireless Society of London and, in 1922, the Radio Society of Great Britain. McMichael founded his company on Wexham Road in June 1920. He developed mobile wireless communications with the railways, won government contracts in 1926 and produced some of the first portable radios to be seen. His 1934 Messenger radio was advertised as 'costing a little more - so much the better'. Later, McMichael's diversified into electronics, but the recession took its toll in 1980.

Above: The newsreels of the late 1930s had made us realise that the next war that touched Britain would be one that would be fought at home as well as abroad. On our cinema screens, we had heard the scream of the dive-bombers and the roar of the Heinkels and Junkers as they poured a rain of death down on Guernica, in 1937, during the civil war in Spain. These sights and sounds had alerted us to the nature of warfare to come. Bomb shelters were erected in gardens and people turned cellars into emergency rooms, should the need to escape from the bombing ever come to our shores. There were Morrison shelters, named after Herbert Morrison, who was Home Secretary during the war. Given free to needy families, they could also be bought for £7. As they were little more than a reinforced cage into which you could crawl whilst staying indoors, they did not catch on too well. More popular were the Anderson shelters. Where possible, it was sensible to erect them away from housing. Those in gardens were too close to the action, but, in built up areas, that was easier said than done. War has only just broken out, but the finishing touches are being applied to this Anderson shelter. Designed to keep a family safe, it is being covered with earth. This will act as both an extra protection from the shock waves and camouflage from the prying eyes of the bomb aimer above.

Top: It might have come as a shock to even the most knowledgeable of these members of the Slough Division of St John Ambulance Brigade to discover that their roots were in the 11th century. It was a time of the religious crusades to the Holy Land. Disease was more likely to be a killer than any Saracen's scimitar. It was in 1099 that the Knights Hospitaliers of St John set up a military hospital in Palestine. It could cater for over 2,000 patients. It was from the era of Richard the Lionheart that the corps developed. No soccer match or large concert would be complete nowadays without the dark uniforms and white sashes of the St John Ambulance team being present. On hand to lend first aid and help at the first sign of a broken limb on the field or a case of hysteria in the audience, these well trained folk could also be found at village fetes and summer shows. Tending to a touch of sun was well within their brief. In the war they played an even more important part. St John's was a branch of the civil defence that would sweep into action during the Blitz, when there were casualties to be tended and relatives to be comforted. Those were dangerous times and the members responded magnificently, with little thought for their own safety. Tin hats and gas masks became a necessary part of the uniform. Any vehicle would do as a makeshift ambulance. This laundry van, probably a part of one member's normal daytime occupation, was ideal for the job. Instead of 'nu-life' for costumes and suits, it could be a saved life for a bomb victim.

Bottom: The death of the role stereotype began in the World War I. Millions of men were in the trenches. Someone had to drive the trams, milk the cows and work in the munitions factories. Women stepped into the breach and you could be forgiven for thinking that war had more impact on equality than Mrs Pankhurst. When the soldiers returned home, they found that their wives and sweethearts were not going to let go of their degree of freedom without a struggle. When World War II came along, it came as no surprise to see the so-called weaker sex taking over again. Women made up one third of all the service and civilian personnel who were involved in the war. They brought in the harvest, ran the forces' operations rooms and took their places on the assembly lines. Manufacturing and engineering would have ground to a halt without them. After all that, they still found time to run the house and bring up the children. These young women became highly skilled in the construction of Hurricane aircraft. It was their ability to put together a reliable and effective fighter plane for the defence of the realm. The young men who flew them took for granted that the workmanship was 'ace'. They should have acknowledged the 'workwomanship'. The first production line Hawker Hurricane took to the skies in 1937. It was the first RAF plane to exceed 300 mph. In their first year of the war, the Hurricanes shot down over 1,500 of the enemy. This total was more than that of all the other fighter planes put together, including the famed Spitfire.

Right: The fighter plane is one of the products we would all like to see the back of. Its very existence means that we cannot be sure of peace. So, in 1944, it was with mixed emotions that we waved goodbye to the last of the 14,000 Hurricanes that had been produced. This one was named 'Last of the many'. They had served us well. In the Battle

of Britain they helped see off the Luftwaffe and, being a versatile craft, had been able to undergo some 20 modifications in their short life span. These meant that the aircraft had served as a fighter-bomber, carrier and attack plane. Its versatility saw it capable of flying at 36,000 feet and, later, carry 40 millimetre cannon and bomb and rocket racks. It was in 1936 that Hawker Aircraft Ltd came to Langley and had built its airfield and factory by 1938. At the height of its production, in 1942, the factory was producing five planes per day. Luck played a part as only a handful of bombs ever fell close by, during the whole of the war. Just in case, there was always a Hurricane ready and waiting on the runway. Should the Luftwaffe have threatened, it was prepared to be scrambled at a moment's notice. Other aircraft manufactured at Langley included the Tempest, Typhoon, Fury and Sea Fury. By 1950, the airfield was not big enough to cope with newer and larger machines. The site was leased to the Ford Motor Company.

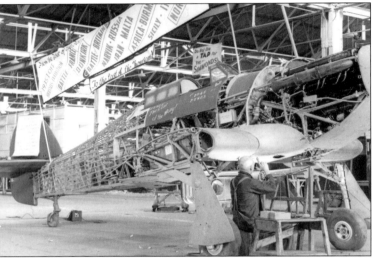

The old timer must have wondered what he had fought for. In 1914 he marched off to war with the words, 'back home for Christmas' ringing in his ears. He had been told that the war to end all wars would leave Britain a proud, prosperous and peaceful nation. How he had been misled. Here, in the midst of another world war, he has had to come to rely on handouts to help him manage. Was this the land fit for heroes for which he and his pals had struggled through the mud of Ypres and the Somme? Miss D Blunden of the Women's Voluntary Service (WVS) looks anxiously towards him as she joins with her colleagues distributing tins of food to the needy. Throughout the war, the WVS collected clothing food and other vital supplies to help those who had suffered from the shortages brought on by the difficulties of wartime. This was not a band of do-gooders, but an active unit in the civil defence. The women of the WVS were out on the streets when the bombs were falling, setting up mobile canteens and shelters for those made homeless by Goering's bombers. They supported the firefighters and rescue services, with little regard for their own safety. The organisation was set up by Lady Stella Reading in 1938. Recognising that war was inevitable, the WVS ran first aid and gas defence classes for civilians. After the war, it continued to give assistance in times of disaster, such as the East Coast floods in 1953. In 1966, shortly after helping at the Aberfan tragedy, it became the Women's Royal Voluntary Service.

Above: The V for victory placard is proudly held up as a backdrop to the party. It was right that it should be. Britain had sacrificed enough during World War II. Unlike the Great War of 1914-18, this had been one that had brought destruction and suffering to civilians as well as the military. Towns and cities had been bombed repeatedly, though Britain had fared better than most. About seven per cent of its housing had been destroyed, but that was enough to affect everyone. We all had a relative who had been the object of the Luftwaffe strikes. Estimates put British and Commonwealth losses at 500,000 military and 80,000 civilian. No wonder these residents of Loddon Spur on Oatlands Drive wanted to show their joy that there was light at the end of the six year tunnel. The trestles were pulled out and every chair that could be crammed into the spaces along the tables was used. Britons love to dress up, whether it is in costume or our best glad rags. What better excuse was there than the thought of a peace that would see us out and our children into old age. That was the hope in September 1945. We were celebrating VE day a little late, but, no matter, there would be VJ day to come. The Japanese had surrendered in August and there were POWs from that side of the world to welcome home.

Above right: The victory flags are held proudly, as the VJ celebrations at Trafalgar Place in old Windsor are about to start. It is a nice early autumnal afternoon in September 1945. Buns and cakes are waiting to be scoffed. First, we must pose for the camera to take the picture that will

stand on the sideboard or on the mantel above the fire for many a long year. Little posies of flowers decorate the table and the children have put on their Sunday best. This is a special day and must be honoured with a sense of occasion as well as merriment. The adults take one side and the kiddies the other. The collars and ties worn by the lads puts the photo into a time when this was how you were turned out for an important function. No training shoes and T-shirts here. The little girls had their hair neatly cropped and swept to the side. Kirby grips and hair slides held everything in place. It had to be done just so, even down to the freshly laundered tablecloth. It is a sobering thought to realise who are missing from this snap. There are no young men. They are still making their way home from the battlefield. Some of them will not be making it back and Britain will, for a time, be a place for women, the old and the young when the dust has settled. In the meantime, pass the fairy cakes round.

There had not been a great deal to celebrate during the previous six years. The war had dragged on and seemed as if it would never end. By 1945, the future began to look a little brighter. Our boys overseas were heading across Europe and into Germany. There was still the occasional blip as the Nazi doodlebugs made their way across the Channel. Then, in early summer came the wonderful news. The war in Europe was over. Hitler was dead and our country was free from the threat of the jackboot. We could look forward to the day when our loved ones would return from the front. Sadly, there were some who would not make it. Around this table were wives and children who might not see their husbands or fathers again. However, they could all join together to show that famous British bulldog spirit. If anyone knew how to party, it was us. Streets up and down the land rejoiced that freedom had been won. There were parties galore, just like this one on Waterbeach Road, near Granville playing field. Mr and Mrs Bowyer sit proudly at the head of the table, waiting for the festivities to begin. Look how patiently the children wait for the bowls of jelly and ice cream to be passed round. Soon, little faces will be smeared with all manner of good things. Why not? At last we had something to cheer about. Parties like these are to celebrate the future, as well as the past. That future belongs to the little ones.

As good as gold and worth twice as much, the little tots of Salt Hill Way are about to enjoy their street party. The youngest of children would not realise how important it was in all our lives that victory had been won in 1945. The German domination in Europe had been broken and it was time to let down our hair and have the sort of good time that had been denied to us for so long. The older children would know that soon dad would be home from the war and that family life could start again. In years to come they would reminisce about the party they had to join in with the rest of the free world's celebrations. These kiddies will be grandparents by now. They will never have grown tired of sitting their grandchildren on their knees and telling of that day. How could they forget that they dressed up and laughed without a care for the first time in ages? There were some smashing costumes, as well. Mum had gone to an awful lot of trouble in running up Mickey Mouse ears from some bits of blackout curtaining that would not be needed again. There were some belting outfits, too. Look at the little lad at the front, with the round stomach and large black rimmed specs. He did not know that he was supposed to be Ernest Bevin, the Minister of Labour, during the war. Whether or not the lad won a prize, we do not know. His mum should have done, for the idea.

Shopping spree

Below: The locals got used to the hoardings at Crown Corner. They first appeared in 1925. No temporary measure, they stayed in place until 1938. In that year the Prudential Buildings went up and remain there today. The lamppost in the centre of the crossroads was powered by electricity, but, in 1934, older residents could remember when gas was used for street lighting. They would have to have been very old to remember the first lamps. It was as far back as 1849 when High Street was illuminated by gaslight. The A332 takes you south to Windsor from this corner and north, left in front of the hoardings, led along William Street towards the railway line. This part of Britain must have been hot stuff. The Palace was showing a fabulous double bill, 'Spanish Passion' coupled with 'The Temptress'. These days, our grandparents are always criticising the sordid nature of so many movies and TV programmes. They must have forgotten about this pair of blockbusters that hit Slough in 1934. Even in

Windsor, at the Theatre Royal, they were at it as well. 'Our Lodger' probably got up to a trick or two that should be kept away from delicate ears. Let us hope that the good parishioners of St Ethelbert's, behind the hoardings, did not pass this way on their way to Sunday Service. It would have been better to spare their blushes.

Bottom: The hoardings at Crown Corner were there for most of the years between the two world wars. The photograph was taken in the early 1930s with a view northeast along William Street. The old London to Bath road runs across the bottom of the picture. Bill posting was a form of fairly cheap of advertising that continued right through the 20th century. The style changed, but the intention was still the same - promote the product. Later posters would shock, amuse or titillate. Those in the 30s tended just to be informative. Behind the men in front of the advert for Player's Navy Cut, there is part of the slogan to be seen. Children were amused to be told that cigarettes went 'one, two, three, four... because 'it is the tobacco that counts'. Behind the hoardings and in front of St Ethelbert's Church, were the buildings of Slough Farm. In the 19th century, farming was important to the area. There was a cattle market in Slough for most of the 20th century. The town is close to rich soil and land that drains well. Cippenham Court Farm and Riding Court Farm were major agricultural centres a century ago. Although there is little to be seen of this rural past in Slough now, farming is still carried on in Eton Wick, Dorney and Wexham. The farmhouse on Slough Farm was called 'The Cedars'. It was converted to become the district council offices in 1908.

Above: Part of the Thames valley is known as England's Silicon Valley. Modern computer and technology companies can be found on the Trading Estate. But, Slough has never been behind the times in seeking to use the very latest in gadgetry and hi-tech developments. In the late 1930s, our homes were blessed with the latest wizardry of that age. Dad did not have to shove the old push me pull you lawn mower across the grass. There was now an electric one that eased the backbreaking job. Mum had her vacuum cleaner, or Hoover as we all called it, and a washing machine instead of the dolly tub. Getting down on your hands and knees to shine the floor was no longer a problem. There was even an electric floor polisher available. Not all of us could afford them, but Fleet Electrics could arrange 'tick' to help spread the payments. Burton proudly displayed its impressive Oxford Street address above the shop window as a sign that its trousers and jackets were of capital quality. Above was the Central Billiards Club, where many a misspent youth was had trying to match the plants, cannons and in-offs of the mighty Fred and Joe Davis. At one time, to get a drink in the Reindeer, you had to go in through the yard at the back. It first saw the light of day in 1618 and was rebuilt in 1934. Burton Tailors stands on the site of that old yard.

Above right: This view of the Prudential Buildings on the corner of William Street was taken around 1938. The magnificent sweep of the building is one that town planners have happily left alone. It would have been a crying shame to do away with such a grand sight. The area was first mapped in 1773, but the earliest remaining picture of Slough is a painting by John Nixon. It dates from 1801. There were inns and houses clustered around this crossroads, the first centre of the town, as we know it now. The peasant centre would have been in Stoke Poges,

rather than down in Upton cum Chalvey. By 1900, the scene here would have included the Red Lion Inn, a wine merchant and the Clock House refreshment rooms. The Red Lion was another of Slough's coaching inns and did a roaring trade in attending to thirsty and hungry passengers, as well as the local population that frequented its bars. By the 1920s, the importance of the Red Lion, along with so many other of its type, had gone. The stagecoaches no longer existed, consigned to a place in history by the railway and the motor car. The Red Lion disappeared, too. For a while, it had strange competition from a Temperance Hotel. The movement had gained ground in the 19th century. Church leaders and charity workers had become appalled at the poverty brought to families by the demon drink. Wage packets were thin enough without the housekeeping being poured into the landlord's pockets. The Temperance Hotel offered food, accommodation and a place to relax away from the temptations of John Barleycorn.

Right: In the distance, towards Sussex Place and the old line of the Bath Road (A4), are some of the oldest surviving buildings on the High Street. They go back to the late 17th century and were known as Regent's Place. All the way along the full stretch of the High Street, modern Slough has a mixture of the old and new. Many of the buildings on the northern side have a history to them, but those to the south are mainly from the 1970s and 1980s. On the corner of the Grove in the 1950s, the domed Methodist Central Hall still stood, looking across the way to the Slough Co-operative Stores. The Co-op boasted that it was 'the largest retailer in town', with a turnover of £1.6m. That was a tidy sum in those days. The first fully organised Co-op had been set up in 1844, by the Rochdale Society of Equitable Pioneers. The society created a set of organisational and working rules that were widely adopted. They included open membership, democratic control, no religious or political discrimination, sales at prevailing market prices and the setting aside of some earnings for education. The Rochdale Co-op opened in a little shop in Toad Lane. For about 50 years, during Victorian times, there had been several co-operative types of movements in and around Slough. It was not until 1892 that Slough Co-op opened its doors at 190 High Street, opposite Turner's famous nursery. It expanded quickly, taking over the shop next door in 1894.

Below: It is a quiet time for a change. The hurry and scurry that was to become the norm for the High Street was still a few years away. Looking east, the Prudential Buildings hold centre stage in the distance. There is little reason to be out and about on the street. The war is still upon us and petrol rationing means a quiet time on the roads. We also had to use coupons to buy our food. There was only so much to go around and those coupons were jealously guarded as mum worked out her budget for the week. It was all very well to have the house-keeping money, but, if there was little butter to be had or clothing to be sold, there was not much point coming into town. The butcher became everyone's friend. Fifty years later you could watch TV and see Coronation Street's Fred Elliott. His character was based on the old family butcher who would always put a bit on the side for his favourite, and usually prettiest, customers. He had to have a sense of humour and, like Corporal Jones, in Dad's Army, be something of a character, as well. These were hard times for everyone and the shopkeepers of Slough felt the pinch. Few people on the street or coming into their places of business meant that the cash registers did not jangle. Clothes were made at home and vegetable plots sprang up in most gardens. Many a shop did not survive; another victim of Herr Hitler.

The traffic lights glow green to signal that the bus can move on towards London Road. The following row of lorries and cars show what a crawl this 1958 journey had become. There were still nearly 20 miles for the double decker to cover before it would reach its destination. The 97 horse power omnibus that Flanders and Swann sang about in their revue, 'At the drop of a hat', was a sight almost unique to the British. Even in these days of deregulation and little minibuses nipping around the streets, there is still a special place in our hearts and memory banks when we see one of these 'proper buses' come into

view. As children, we would collect bus tickets and the ends of the roll that the conductor would let us have. We would cheek the clippie, until she had taken enough and threatened to clip our ears instead of our tickets. Smokers could puff away to their heart's content on the upper deck. Heaven help you, though, if the inspector got on and found you had bought a tuppenny ticket for a tanner's ride! It is little wonder that one of the best loved TV comedies of the late 60s and 70s was 'On the buses'. The antics of Reg Varney and Stephen Lewis kept us in tucks.

Above: The Prudential Buildings still stand at Crown Corner. Different shops can be seen there today. At the end of the 1990s there were fast food and kebab shops. There was also a computer games shop, selling the latest PC and Play-Station software. Here, in the 1950s, a computer was something you read about in the Eagle as Dan Dare rocketed off to do battle with his arch enemy, the Mekon. Health scares about smoking and bans on advertising were s long way off. 'You're never alone with a Strand' was an acceptable message to come to us on the TV in the late 60s. Here we are being given the urge to smoke those little cigars that were so popular, Manikins. Filter tipped Craven A cigarettes even promised that you should switch to them 'for your throat's sake'. Wills' Whiffs and rough shag tobacco had a lovely smell as you went into the tobacconist. He would mix you a special from black Sobranie or Turkish imports. Granddad enjoyed cutting a plug of thick twist and ramming it into his battered old briar, horning it in with his calloused thumb. It seems ironic, now, that just along the block is the chemist's. There our smoker could get a packet of Zubes to ease his dry throat. He probably did not stop to think that the cause of his discomfort lay in what he had just bought next door. Why does the devil have the best tunes? The aroma of pipe smoke or the scent of the raw tobacco is so attractive, yet it does so much harm. Another sign of the times is the pointer to the public conveniences. What a longwinded way to say 'loo'.

Above right: This artist's impression of the Queensmere development was produced in 1965. This decade and the following 70s brought many changes to the town as the face of old Slough was redeveloped. The 1930s had brought the first housing estates that were filled with workers from the new factories. After the war, even more housing was put up to meet the shortage created by bombing and building restrictions that were only relaxed in peacetime. Both

Slough Borough Council and London County Council provided the funding for the new estates. Wexham Court, Britwell and Langley were all developed. But it was the 1960s that saw the town itself in change. In 1965, Wexham Park Hospital was built. The dual carriageway was begun in 1967 to relieve the pressure on High Street. But, it was in the 1970s that the centre of Slough changed forever. So much so that some visitors thought it was one of the new towns. The older buildings disappeared. Chandos Street was no more. The Post Office, Public Hall, Drill Hall and Fire Station were either gone or replaced elsewhere. In 1972, the building of Queensmere was begun on the north side of High Street. There is now no need to venture outside its walls in order to fulfil a person's shopping needs. Food, clothing and leisure shops are all here, along with the major department stores. The developers were ahead of their time in making sure that the Queensmere kept part of the history of Slough alive. Some of the old place and street names are used for the centre's malls.

At work

Leslie McMichael was a pioneer in radio operation and development. Although the portable radios his company produced in the late 1920s and 1930s were the size of small suitcases, they were the forerunner of the 'trannie' of the 1960s and the mini Walkman of today. The company had only been set up for five years when this 1925 scene of the assembly bay was captured. Already, there was a workforce numbering scores of men and women, putting together the complex mixture of wiring, valves and speakers. The modern circuit board seems so much easier; just a quick dab with the soldering iron and the job's done. The possibilities of radio had been recognised by the English physicist Michael Faraday. He demonstrated that an electrical current could produce a magnetic field. In 1864 James Clerk Maxwell, a professor of experimental physics at Cambridge, proved mathematically that these electrical disturbances could be detected at considerable distances. McMichael's interest was awakened before the first world war, but sound broadcasting did not really begin as an entertainment until around 1920. He was in on the ground floor. When the BBC was born in 1922, McMichael used the boom in national interest to good effect. The population was gripped with the idea of listening to news, stories and music coming directly into their living rooms. Families gathered together for an evening's entertainment around the 'wireless'. The assembly bay at McMichael's worked flat out to keep up with the orders that flooded in.

Bosses, foremen, shop floor workers, wives and sweethearts are ready to share the fun of the works outing. With a crate of brown ale on the back seat and a warning from the killjoys not to make fools of themselves, this happy bunch from G Case and Son was ready and raring to go. In the early 1930s, the destination of the day out to the seaside was little changed from what it would be today. Bournemouth, Brighton and Eastbourne all had their attractions. The Windsorian coach made the journey on countless occasions in that and every summer. For the rest of the week the workforce had busied itself in the wireless dealers on Grove parade. Now was the time to let their hair down. After a day at the coast, it would be fish and chips and a singsong on the way back home. If the boss was feeling generous, he would have put his hand in his pocket and made sure the crate the lads had got was matched with another one in the boot. Three cheers for him and a rousing chorus of 'For he's a jolly good fellow' would let him know how much the gesture was appreciated. The coach driver, seen on the right, would hope that after the strains of 'The sun has got his hat on', belted out from the back seat, certain niceties and customs would be observed. A whip round for the driver was always a feature of these outings.

Below: A quarter of a century before Buddy Holly sang 'Oh boy' on record, the phrase was well known on the Slough Trading Estate. This brand of chewing gum had crossed the Atlantic and become established as one of the hundreds of companies that would set up home there from the 1920s onwards. The management was careful about hygiene and the workers producing Oh-boy wore protective coats. The women had to have their hair tucked under their caps to avoid any contamination. Around 1930, no-one blinked an eye at the advert for Pick-a-ninny sweets, but such a brand name would be economic suicide in today's climate. Older locals despised the chewing gum that the company produced, but youngsters had seen films from Hollywood. Smart Americans chewed on their gum and British youth, both before and after the war, liked to ape what was new and trendy from the other side of the 'big pond'. The habit was copied from the Red Indians, who chewed spruce resin. Americans used chicle, from the sapodilla tree, instead. After World War II, various waxes, plastics and synthetic rubber replaced chicle.

The factory was built on the site of a district that was known as 'the Dump'. During World War I a repair depot for military vehicles was set up in Cippenham. Some 600 acres of land between Bath Road and Farnham Road were allocated, but the depot was not finished when the war ended. Broken down vehicles littered the waterlogged ground. Then the Slough Trading Company came to take it over and the estate began.

Men spend almost as much on toiletries as do women. They hog the bathroom before they go out for the evening and go to hair stylists when once a short back and sides at the barber was enough. Lads in the 1950s coated their hair with Brylcreem and in the 60s started to use conditioner on their long hair. By the 70s, boxer Henry Cooper and soccer star Georgie Best were advising men to 'splash it all over' with aftershave. Deodorant just for men appeared on the shelves in the 1980s, but what were attitudes like round about 1934? The packing department at Northam Warren, on the Trading Estate, has row upon row of women boxing up little bottles of Odo-ro-no. That, and its big rival, Mum Rollette, dominated the deodorant

By the 70s, Henry Cooper and George Best were advising men to 'splash it all over' with aftershave

field for several decades in the mid 20th century. These were products for women. They did not sweat, of course, but merely perspire. Perfumes and deodorants were to the Elizabethans a means of disguising the smell of unwashed bodies. The 20th century woman was a cleaner being, but she still wanted something that would prevent the unsightly stain under the armpit and the stale smell that went with it. Men were made of different stuff back then. Whilst the occasional male would confess to a dab of after-shave, sweaty armpits were manly, a sure sign of honest toil. Daring to admit to using the missus' roll-on; that would have seen him branded as 'a big Jessie'.

Below: Slough Station had been standing for some 70 years at this time. Designs were begun in 1882 and it opened for business in 1884. The famous designer and engineer, Isambard Kingdom Brunel, was responsible for one of the earlier rebuilds of the station. The road leading to the station was named Brunel Way, in his honour. He was a leading light in the field of transport design. As well as railways and bridges, he was responsible for three of Britain's most famous ships, the Great Eastern, Great Britain and the Great Western. It was he who decided that the best route from Paddington to Bristol was via Slough. As engineer to the Great Western Railway, he saw the railways come to the town in 1838. The first stretch of line, as far as Taplow, was opened in 1838. Not everyone approved of the new form of transport. Owners of private roads, the Colnbrook Turnpike Trust in particular, resented this intrusion into its near monopoly on public transport. The effect on their tolls was to be devastating. Even the Provost of Eton objected as he thought the railway would impact

on the morals of schoolboys and encourage them to run away to the bright lights of London! Queen Victoria was made of stronger stuff. She took her first train ride from Slough, in 1842. The first Slough Station opened in 1840, two years after it had been given a rail service! The photographed station was remodelled internally in 1938.

Bottom: In the middle of the 19th century, James Elliman Senior established a draper's business on the newly built Buckingham Place. Very soon he had started to sell his own patent embrocation. The first sales were made in 1847. It was a secret mixture of eggs, turpentine and vinegar. The damp housing that people lived in and the hard physical work they performed both contributed to aches, pains and rheumatism. They used Elliman's Embrocation as a rub to ease those aching limbs. The embrocation was widely used on animals. Horses benefited from a good old rubbing down with the magic mixture. James Elliman took over the business from his father in 1870. Although the techniques used in production were fairly basic, Elliman's advertising was lively. 'An excellent good thing' was how he promoted the product and even used an early form of strip cartoon in the sales drive. The young packer and labeller in the 1960 picture might not need to use embrocation for his creaky joints, but countless others came to rely on it being manufactured on Chandos Street. The company moved here in 1882. Elliman's was taken over by Horlicks in 1961, but Beechams continued the line when it came under this firm's banner in 1970. The younger Elliman was a great benefactor. He donated much of his wealth in providing such amenities as the Public Hall, Mackenzie Street Fire Station and Salt Hill Playing Fields. His name lives on in Elliman Avenue and the James Elliman School.

Life is sweet on Mars

To the people of Slough, Mars Confectionery needs no introduction. The company is well-known throughout the area as a successful, well-managed business, and as a good employer committed to the training and development of all its 'associates' (the company's term for its workforce). Its products are, of course, famous the world over. We all have our own particular favourites; all the chocolate bars we have known and loved since our childhood seem to come out of the Mars factory - not only the MARS bar, but MILKY WAY, GALAXY, SNICKERS, MALTESERS, TOPIC, BOUNTY and TWIX. For those of us who prefer a fruity flavour there are STARBURST fruit sweets, and when we have a sore throat TUNES or LOCKETS are a great comfort.

The great British public began to acquire its taste for MARS bars in August 1932. Mr Forrest Mars Senior rented a small factory on the Slough Trading Estate and on August Bank Holiday Monday the very first bars were produced by hand. The MARS bar, with its nougat and caramel and thick, rich milk

Below: The first MARS wrapper, 1932.
Bottom: A group of associates who joined the company in 1932.

chocolate, was new and unique, and proved so popular that within a year or so the workforce had grown from 12 to 100.

From the very outset, the company was run along highly professional lines. Photographs taken in 1932 show associates who worked in the factory wearing white overalls; guidelines on the different methods of working chocolate were produced and distributed; and a lively and highly imaginative approach to marketing was adopted. Among the various early incentives which encouraged retailers to display Mars products were competitions, free gifts, and the promise of a visit from the Guineas Man who toured round the shops and gave away a guinea (£1-1s-0d) to the ones which featured a prominent display of Mars goods. Early advertising set the standard

Above centre (both pictures): *Early MARS advertisements.*
Top: *Outside the loading bay in March 1933.*

for the long succession of memorable advertising campaigns which followed. Before the days of television, eye-catching advertisements appeared on posters, in shop windows, in magazines and even on the back covers of paperbacks, and over the years many Mars slogans have imprinted themselves indelibly on the memory. Who doesn't know 'A MARS a day helps you work, rest and play'?

In 1935 Mars introduced its second chocolate bar, MILKY WAY, followed in 1936 by MALTESERS. During the war years, however, production was interrupted and many Mars associates were called up for active service. Meanwhile a skeleton staff at Slough helped keep up morale both at home and amongst the armed forces overseas by keeping up production of MARS bars. Alongside the production line, bacon and Red Cross parcels were packed for the troops, while another part of the factory became a military transport store. When peace returned the factory was completely

modernised; new machinery and equipment was introduced, and in 1947 the company launched its first sugar confectionery - SPANGLES.

It was around this time that Mars formalised its business philosophies in a company handbook called 'This is Mars'. At the same time a new pension plan was introduced which provided better benefits, a doctor was appointed, cafeteria facilities improved and a company newsletter was launched. Mars' caring attitude towards its associates, at a time when many employers were offering minimal benefits, received a good deal of attention from industry at large. Meanwhile its products were receiving a gratifying amount of attention from the public at large; the 'Eagle' comic ran a series of Mars cartoons in 1950, and in 1955 Mars was able to run its first television adver-

tising, using such famous personalities as Bob Monkhouse and Petula Clark to prove that 'Stars love MARS'.

Above: *To cope with growth Mars recruited more associates. This advertisement was taken from the Slough, Eton and Windsor Observer in February 1952.* ***Top:*** *The machine which sealed the ends of the MARS wrapper in the 1940s.* ***Left:*** *And another thing...SPANGLES were a popular favourite of children as this 1950s advertising promotion shows.*

STARBURST). In the 1980s the MARS bar became the first confectionery brand to reach sales of £100 million.

Today, Mars Confectionery in Slough employs aound 2,200 associates. It is part of Mars, Incorporated, a privately owned business employing 30,000 people throughout the world. Mars, Inc's annual sales are in excess of US $13 billion dollars and over a third of the chocolate bars sold around the world are made by Mars.

In Slough, Mars' two factories produce over 200,000 tonnes of confectionery each year - including 3 million MARS bars every day. The MARS bar continues to be the UK's best selling single bar.

Sweet rationing had finally ended in the Spring of '53. Production was back in full swing, and with all its existing products permanently established as household names, Mars began to expand its range. More associates were employed, both in the factory and on the sales team. Female shift-workers could expect to take home at least £7 a week, which in 1954 was an excellent rate of pay, and in addition the benefits package was extremely comprehensive, including as it did a non-contributory pension scheme, two weeks' annual paid holiday, air-conditioning, and 'music while you work'!

In 1961 a second factory was built in Slough, primarily to make sugar confectionery. Production subsequently increased by over 250 per cent during the 60s and 70s, and many new products were introduced which went on to become household names - TOPIC, TWIX, REVELS, GALAXY, MARATHON (now SNICKERS) and OPAL FRUITS (now

Over the years we have grown used to enjoying our favourite Mars products in a number of novel guises - in multi-packs, as minis, and as ice-cream. The spirit of innovation which has been at the heart of the company since Forrest Mars Senior started the business will always find ways to express itself, in new products like CELEBRATIONS or new packaging, catchy advertising slogans, and pro-active personnel and organisation policies aimed at enhancing the working environment. Acknowledged by experts as one of the world's best-managed companies, Mars is regarded as one of Britain's best employers. 'Good products plus good people makes a good business" was one of Forrest Mars Senior's guidelines for running the company he founded. It is a formula to which Mars has always adhered.

Top left: *A cinema influenced advertisement.*
Above: *Around 3 million MARS bars are made every day in Slough.* **Left:** *CELEBRATIONS, launched in 1997, is now the most popular boxed chocolate in the UK.*

Keeping business and industry running smoothly, even when the going gets tough

It is sometimes said that the single invention which has done most to change the course of the history of mankind is the wheel. If this is so, then the relative importance of the development of the perfect castor should not be under-estimated. In today's culture of labour-saving devices and sound ergonomic designs, we take it for granted that heavy items will come ready provided with the means of shifting them if necessary. On the whole our furniture, both at home and at work, has become lighter and more practical over the last sixty years or so. Certainly the heavy mahogany or walnut sideboards, couches, armchairs and tables which filled the average household's dining room and drawing room would have caused the housewives and housemaids of the period many a headache - or backache - had it not been for the invention of castors.

In the mid-thirties, many items of furniture were fitted with castors made by a company called Suvretta Furnitures Limited, based at 168 Regent Street, London. Founded on 14th April 1934 by Mr W R

Goldstein and Mr Marcel Menko, who had previously been engaged in jointly running a Swiss castor agency, the company's first product was a patent sprung version of the castor, designed by Mr Goldstein. This interested many furniture manufacturers, and the new firm experienced a healthy growth in business. It made smooth-running castors for domestic items such as dinner wagons, tea trolleys, cocktail cabinets, baby cots, light moveable furniture and washing machines; it made elegant glass gliders for

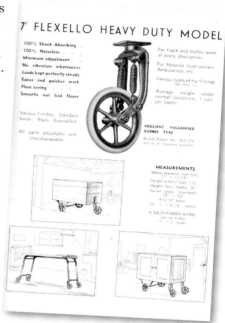

Top left: Mr Bertie Menko, Export Manager.
Above: A page from an early Flexello catalogue.
Below: Loading castors for export onto a truck.

radiograms, sideboards, armchairs, settees, divans, tables and tallboys; it made castors with optional brake attachments for hospital furniture, bedsteads, food carriers and ambulance use; it made a limited range of extra heavy castors for trucks and trolleys. In 1938 the company changed its name to Flexello Limited and moved out to Slough, setting up a factory on Bath Road, on the Slough Trading Estate. Here it continued to concentrate initially on its range of castors for its traditional furniture market, but after a while it began to expand its range of heavy duty castors for industry. Having embarked upon this path, the company's next step was to investigate in more detail the particular demands of different sectors of industry; this, of course, led to the identification of a wide variety of specific requirements; and this in turn led to a corresponding expansion and diversification in its range of high quality products.

During the war years Flexello, at Slough, concentrated on essential war work for the Ministry of Defence.

When peace returned the company resumed its pursuit of new marketplaces for its innovative products, and succeeded so well that it became the largest castor manufacturer in Europe at that time. Then in the mid-50s, with the opening up of the export market, it was able to compound its success at home with a significant increase in export sales. Bertie Menko, Marcel Menko's cousin, had by this time joined the company and taken up the position of Export Sales Manager. Seeing the possibilities for global expansion that lay ahead, Flexello set up a subsidiary venture whose specific purpose was to develop opportunities overseas, and within a few years its products had found a market in more than 60 countries worldwide.

The business had come a long way in its first 25 years, and this was highlighted at the end of the 60s when, following a decade of rapid expansion, Flexello was floated on the stock market. Although the Menko

Above: *Flexello headquarters.*
Below: *Working capstans in the Machine Shop.*

family no longer owned the business, the contribution of successive generations, which over the years was such a very important factor in its success, was to continue for a further 20 years. Bertie Menko was awarded an MBE during his time with the company, and Marcel Menko's son gave invaluable service as Director and later Chairman. As a public company, however, Flexello was in a stronger financial position and continued to grow throughout the 70s, remaining constantly alert to new opportunities. In 1977 an additional factory was opened at Highworth, near Swindon, to specialise in injection and polyurethane moulding for the manufacture of nylon and polyurethane wheels; subsequently this temporarily became the home for the machine shop and later for the sales and distribution divisions, before being closed in 1993.

When the recession began to affect British industry during the 80s, international trade became even more crucial to the company's continued success, and in 1981 Flexello opened a marketing

Right: *The Assembly Shop on Bath Road.* **Below:** *The Buffing Shop, where castors go before chroming.*

company in Australia to handle the growing trade with the thriving South-East Asian markets. Ten years later, in an economic climate which was becoming increasingly dominated by giant multinationals, Flexello joined forces with Japan's foremost manufacturer of castors, becoming a wholly owned subsidiary of the Nansin Company Limited. The strengths of these two major manufacturers complemented each other perfectly; Flexello's global marketing skills combined with Nansin's expertise in automated manufacturing to

create an immensely capable, efficient and progressive organisation. Up to the time of the merger, the output of the Slough factory was to a large extent manually produced, but shortly afterwards the company, under its recently-appointed Managing Director Mr

Above: The King and Queen of Denmark showing a keen interest in the Flexello Castors stand at the Copenhagen British Exhibition in 1948.
Top: The Press Shop.

Taniguchi, embarked on a massive investment programme to upgrade machinery and take the factory forward into a new era of automation. Some £6million was ploughed into the business, and the capacity of the factory was effectively doubled.

In the midst of this exciting period of growth and restructuring, Flexello's lease on the Bath Road premises ran out, and it was time to move. The company had already investigated the various options open to it. Although in theory its manufacturing base could be relocated to any town of its choosing, there were a number of advantages in staying in Slough; the main one was, of course, that the business was well-established there, and also that it was the home of the firm's loyal and experienced workforce, now fully trained on the new machinery. Flexello had therefore approached Slough Estates with a view to identifying available sites in Slough, and was greatly impressed by their helpful and co-operative attitude. In the event Slough Estates played an active part in finding the plot of land in Edinburgh Avenue which was to become Flexello's new home, on a 25 year lease.

The company approached the complex and all-important task of designing a brand-new factory to meet all its present and future needs very carefully. Much of the development was planned around the machinery; but in addition to the actual installation of machinery and equipment, issues to be resolved ranged from power and lighting, heating and ventilation, automatic doors and a fire alarm which gives visual as well as audible warning, to a 'white light' working environment which is better for the workforce, and the provision of energy monitoring systems to enable the company to break down overall running costs and identify possible future savings. Building services consultants ADL were appointed to identify the specific challenges involved and deal with every detail.

As the new factory neared completion, plans were made for the transition from Bath Road to Edinburgh Avenue; it was decided that for a three month period production would run simultaneously at both sites in order to achieve a seamless changeover, with the joint works programme co-ordinated by computer links between the two sites.

The official opening ceremony was held on 12th July 1996. More than 200 people, including a delegation from the parent company in Japan, visited the impressive new factory, and the occasion was seen by many as a virtual re-launch of the company. Employees, however,

Right: *The Assembly Shop, Bath Road.*
Below: *Staff training in the 1960s.*

will remember the Family Fun Day, held shortly afterwards, when the Company marked its commitment to its workforce by turning the marquee into a place of entertainment for employees' children while their parents toured their new workplace; they then had an opportunity to show their families round the building and socialise with fellow-employees and their families.

With around a quarter of the 150-strong workforce at Edinburgh Avenue employed in management, sales, purchasing, personnel, computing and technology, the remainder is engaged in the production side of the business, working in the press and assembly, or in the stores, packing and despatching the finished product. Output currently stands at some 150,000 units per

week, or five million units a year, of which between 80 percent and 90 percent is destined for the export market. Over the years Flexello has retained its leading position in the UK as castor manufacturer, and now, with its state-of-the-art manufacturing base making it the most advanced wheel-and-castor production facility in the country, it has a new edge in this highly competitive market place. The company has always been highly regarded for its levels of excellence and high quality, and with virtually all the castor components now made in-house, the strictest quality control systems are applied throughout the manufacturing process to ensure absolute reliability. At the same time, the policy of continuous research and development of products to which the company has adhered for more than 50 years has given it an unsurpassed ability to anticipate the needs of customers and meet their specific requirements. Flexello has recently updated its product portfolio, identifying and filling any gaps, so that the current product range includes castors designed to meet the whole spectrum of materials handling applications; its customer base includes airports and railway stations, the refuse industry, hospitals, supermarkets

and the construction industry. It can, for instance, supply the heavy duty castors required for access towers and moveable scaffolding. It supplies the special castors which help guide supermarket trolleys full of groceries on a straight course, and it has engineered castors to transport cargoes weighing up to 7,000kg. In fact, no challenge ever defeats the full-time research and development team, working in conjunction with universities and R & D operations in Europe.

Flexello will enter the next millennium as a streamlined, progressive company. Operating on a pan-European level, it will continue to pursue its policy of investment applications engineering to bring the customer high-quality, well-designed products. The company's efficient marketing and distribution network will continually find new ways to maximise business opportunities both at home and in the export market; and Slough, with its capacity for high-volume manufacturing, will continue to produce the quality castors that keep all sectors of business and industry running smoothly, the world over.

Top: *Office staff during the 1950s.*
Left: *Flexello today.*

The Slough factory with a colourful past (and present, and future . . .)

In 1919, at the end of the first world war and long before the days of DIY, non-drip paints and the Dulux dog, the long-established varnish maker Naylor Brothers (London) Limited extended its activities into paint manufacture, setting up a factory in Slough on a 30-acre site former brickfield which had been converted for use as the American Corps of Engineers' stores during the war. Meanwhile, many miles to the east in Stowmarket, research was in progress, inspired by work carried out in the USA by Du Pont; its objective was to develop new processes and finishes for use on the production lines of the British automotive industry, and in due course a nitro-cellulose finishing process came onto the market, developed by Nobel Chemical Finishes Limited and marketed as Belco.

Nobels' next step was to arrange for the manufacture of oil-based undercoats for Belco, and the facilities provided by Naylor Brothers' site in Slough were eminently suitable for this purpose. Accordingly, Nobel Chemical Finishes entered into negotiations which ultimately led to their purchase of Naylors, and 1926 saw the start of a decade of consolidation, with the two companies working together to overcome the difficult economic climate of Britain's industrial depression. Substantial investment was committed to research; and in the autumn of 1929 they produced a one-bake undercoat for the motor industry, the factory's first alkyd-based product, followed in 1931 by a very significant breakthrough - the first of the 'Dulux' alkyd-based synthetic finishes, again based on the Du Pont formulation. Dulux paint was first sold to the building trade in Britain in 1932, and was met with some suspicion because it was so obviously different from the lead-based paints to which decorators were accustomed. It was thinner, went further, and dried more quickly. It was also much more durable; but although this last fact was known in theory, decorators, being practical people, were reluctant to believe it without evidence, which in turn would not be forthcoming until they had used the product extensively. Fortunately, architects and specifiers were more disposed to place their faith in

Above left: The cover of ICI's first house journal in 1928. It symbolised the company's ideas for linking employees and management. Below: A training session at Slough Technical Service Station.

theory; so the decorators whom they contracted were compelled to use the new product, and Dulux was able to begin proving itself. By 1939 it was being stocked by a small but growing number of merchants, and it was gradually gaining acceptance as a promising invention.

In the early 1930s the Slough factory also entered into a licensing agreement with the American Paint Company, under which the American Paint Company's products were manufactured at Slough. Increased production brought problems of a new and threatening nature; records from the mid-30s give details of a controversy which almost put an end to paint manufacture at Slough. Market gardeners to the windward side of the factory complained about fumes, and the matter was further exacerbated when the Council built a housing estate on the northern boundary of the works. Pressure was put upon the company, which responded by making preliminary plans to relocate its entire operation to Stowmarket. Fortunately for us all, however, before the company had

committed itself to the move - which was to cost an estimated £500,000 - the Borough Council reconsidered its position and came to the realisation that a factory that employed so much labour should be viewed as a valuable asset to a growing centre of industry. And so the company stayed in Slough, and not long afterwards became part of Imperial Chemical Industries Limited. A further significant acquisition in 1936 was The British Paint and Lacquer Company Limited in Cowley, whose close connections with Morris Motors Limited were to prove of great future benefit to ICI. Then war broke out, and the company's entire management and office staff moved out of central London to join the factory workers at Slough.

This sudden influx of personnel led to cramped working conditions for everybody; additional problems were posed by the shortages of raw materials, as a result of which the

Above: *1950s testing.*

manufacture of Dulux had to be halted between 1939 and 1948; and twice the factory sustained bomb damage. Turnover was maintained throughout, however, and the company played a leading role in organising essential supplies of raw materials and co-operating with other manufacturers to supply scrim paints, camouflage paints and the special finishes needed for tanks and shells. It was also a member of the Aircraft Finishes Group, a group of seven approved firms responsible for meeting the demands for specialised finishes for aircraft. In addition, incidental discoveries that had arisen out of the extensive research carried out at Slough before the war suddenly took on a new importance when they were adapted to special wartime applications; so urea-formaldehyde resins, and later melamine-formaldehyde resins, formed the basis of a lacquer for the interior of

Jerrycans, which was manufactured in very large quantities for Government contracts.

Nobel Chemical Finishes became known as ICI (Paints) Limited in 1940, and by the end of the war further internal reorganisation had established the Slough factory as part of the Paints Division of Imperial Chemical Industries Limited. The Paints Division controlled a total of six factories in Britain, of which Slough was the largest. Production of Dulux was resumed there in 1948 when the raw materials were freely available again, and within four years Dulux had become the leading brand of paint in the professional field. One factor which contributed to this success was that proof of Dulux's durability was now available - it was noticeable that schools and other public buildings which had been painted with Dulux before the war had survived the years of neglect better than the rest. At this time, too, the market for 'do-it-yourself' decorating products was just beginning to open up, as householders increasingly opted to do their own decorating, rather than pay the sometimes prohibitive rates quoted by professional decorators. So there was clearly great potential to turn Dulux into a large-scale market leader; but equally clearly the company had to take great care in devising and implementing a marketing strategy, as it was in effect launching a relatively new product into a newly-developing marketplace.

Not wishing to alienate the trade which formed its traditional customer base, the company cautiously slanted its early advertising towards the decorating professional with the

Above: *Dulux - 1950s style - being transported from the warehouse.*

slogan 'Say Dulux to your decorator.' At the beginning of the DIY movement there were very real fears that it would cause a split within the industry, with the professional craftsmen and the merchants who supplied them refusing to have anything to do with the products which the retailers supplied to the amateurs. In the event this proved not to be a problem, and today the DIY consumer is recognised and valued as an important part of the market for decorating products. But since it was not possible to predict this, the Paint Division's decision to risk alienating the professionals by putting Dulux on the retail market in 1953 was a brave one. Added to that, it was a new venture for the company in that ICI's traditional market consisted mainly of industrial customers and specialist trade outlets who had an in-depth understanding of the products they were buying; the company had never before

sold its products to the public in such a big way, and so had no real experience of promoting its products. Although Dulux was by now well-known within the trade, the general public would have no reason to buy it unless its advantages were brought to their attention through advertising. So the company advertised. They placed black and white pictures and announcements in the press, they put display material up in shops, and they produced colour cards and leaflets for people to take home. All this coincided with the first big surge of DIY customers, and many of them chose Dulux. The company then progressed to full-page colour advertisements in magazines, posters on buses and railway stations, and other more sophisticated sales aids. In 1955 they were responsible for some of the first ever television advertisements for paint. And in 1961 ICI's place in the annals of advertising was assured for ever when the first Dulux Dog made his appearance and instantly won the hearts of the British public, irresistibly epitomising family values in the setting of a warm, welcoming and well-painted household. Fans of these friendly, tousle-headed, loveable Old English Sheepdogs may like to take this opportunity of refreshing their memories of all the dogs they have seen over the years - Dash, Digby, Duke, Tanya, Pickle, Dillon, Boots, Holly, Sebastian - and Thomas, the star of the 1999 Dulux Colour Campaign, whose short, snappy ads are based on the message, 'You find the colour - we'll match it'.

Meanwhile, research was continuing at Slough. A range of emulsions was developed to replace the pre-war 'distemper';

Left: A Battery of paint mixers in the 1950s.
Below: The Slough site in the 1950s. The factory stretches far off the picture to the right.

after a great deal of experimentation this product was based on polyvinyl acetate, rather than an alkyd emulsion. Marketed as Du-Lite (later Dulite), emulsion was produced in a range of colours which corresponded to the Dulux gloss range; in the early 60s the two brands were merged, with both gloss and emulsion being sold under the name Dulux. Brilliant white paint, introduced in the mid-60s, was a notable success, going on to account for a substantial market share of both gloss and emulsion and giving ICI Paints Division some 40 per cent of the entire paints retail market in Britain and about 20 per cent of the trade market.

In the early 70s the DIY and Trade businesses were split so that the company could meet the differing needs of the two markets and concentrate on the increasing importance of Trade. Competition began to grow more aggressive during the decade which followed, but ICI retained its lead; with the marketplace for brilliant white becoming an area which was contested particularly fiercely, ICI launched its range of off-whites with a hint of colour. The competition followed suit, but Dulux retained three-quarters of the market. This has been the pattern ever since; Dulux has been responsible for a series of new products which competitors merely copy. The trade and DIY markets have Dulux to thank for such innovations as Duette, Sonata, Solid Emulsion, Decorator Select, Colour Dimensions tinting, Natural Whites, Heritage, Eggshell (based on low odour solvents), Kitchens and Bathrooms paint, Satinwood, and the Language of Colour concept which helps customers to create co-ordinating colour schemes..

Nor is ICI Paints' innovation limited to the Dulux range. Other decorative paint brands include Glidden, Valentine, Coral, Alba and Colour Your World, while its recent acquisition of Williams Plc added brands including Hammerite, Cuprinol, Polyfilla, and Polycell to its decorative product range, taking ICI into the woodcare, metalcare,

adhesive and filler market. It has also developed a range of coatings for food and drink cans and refinish paints for repairing vehicle paintwork. Its packaging coatings business is a world leader in the specialised market for internal and external coatings for food and beverage cans and other metal containers, and also includes packaging inks and laminating adhesives and coatings for flexible packaging. Its automotive refinish paints are marketed as ICI Autocolour; this leading brand, which is supplied to the professional end user by selected international suppliers, includes the award-winning Aquabase. This is the world's first waterborne automotive refinish basecoat, and won the Queen's Award for Environmental Achievement.

Dulux is also a pioneer of paint recycling. In 1995, as part of its commitment to the environment, it began sponsoring Community Re>Paint schemes. These schemes, which

Above: *Paint leaving the warehouse.*
Top: *A view of the paint filling line.*

involve collecting surplus decorative paint from the public, and re-distributing it amongst 'not for profit' groups and their clients, have been launched all over the UK, down to Bath and up to Scotland, and Dulux has been sponsoring three schemes each year. Part-used cans of paint suitable for domestic application are collected from specified collection points, and are given to charities, community groups and voluntary organisations. The paint is then used in the local community on projects which would not have otherwise have been financially viable, such as brightening up youth clubs, village halls and elderly people's homes. These schemes are run by local environmental and recycling agencies with the support of their Local Authorities, and provide a very positive solution to the problem of disposal of waste paint; the community benefits, and at the same time landfill sites and refuse collectors are freed from the difficult and messy task of disposal.

ICI Paints' commitment to the environment is just one aspect of its positive approach to its role in the community. Along with the rest of ICI, the Slough factory is currently participating in a national initiative, Positive about Disabled People, aimed at improving employment opportunities for disabled people. Many charities have benefited from the fundraising activities of ICI staff, and the company also takes an active educational role. Its series of informative and attractive publications for use in schools provides an introduction to various aspects of paint technology. Schools are also invited to visit the Slough site on regular occasions including as part of the Chemical Industry Association Open Day programme; at the 1998 Open Day, held in September, Slough mounted fascinating and lively displays on topics such as waste reduction on site, energy conservation, the responsible care, occupational health and paint effects. The Open Day was attended by several hundred employees and their families, local residents, local teachers and councillors. In addition special visits were arranged for pupils from Langley Grammar, Slough Grammar, St Josephs, Slough & Eton, Herschel, Westgate and Baylis Court, and altogether some 230 pupils and teachers were involved in plant tours, demonstrations and lectures. For many local youngsters, a visit to ICI Paints at Slough is a unique opportunity to see chemistry in action, and to compare large-scale production with laboratory work. Adults are more likely to be impressed by the standards of safety, health and protection of the environment; ICI Paints adheres strictly to its renowned safety culture.

With 60 manufacturing sites in 25 countries, and selling in over 120 countries, ICI Paints and its products have become household names throughout the world. But its roots have remained firmly planted in the town where it has made paint for 90 years. For as far into the next millennium as it is possible to foresee, Slough will remain home to the whole family of products from ICI Paints. Including the Dog.

Above: *1980s advertising.*
Below: *ICI's Slough plant today.*

Studying where the children of 'luvvies' once lived

Your schooldays are the happiest times of your life. The more that phrase is rammed down the throats of the youngsters of today, the more chance it has of being received by a yawn, at best. The statement usually comes from a maiden aunt who really has memories of being caned black and blue, being put in detention for a hemline that was too short or studying the Punic Wars whilst her mates were off to the Palais for a bop to some Eddie Cochran music. Whilst East Berkshire College will not guarantee to make your days the happiest, it can help you make them amongst the most interesting and rewarding. There are plenty of courses to choose from. There is also a choice of location to study at. There are four main centres under the College umbrella, at Langley, Maidenhead, Windsor and Heathrow. Good road and rail links make all the centres easily accessible and many of the courses run at more than one centre. Since Langley College combined with Windsor and Maidenhead to become the East

Berkshire College in 1992, it has catered for young men and women who are looking to take the next step in their education, whether young or more mature, that will move them that bit closer to their ultimate dream of what they want to be. For some that will come via 'A' level courses designed to get the students into university. For many others, there are qualifications that are geared specifically towards employment. Most of the tutors have worked in industry and so understand the needs of both the employer and employee.

As well as the academic subjects, there are vocational courses in business, construction, engineering, caring, health and beauty, leisure, travel and tourism. Future stock market whiz kids may, even now, be passing into an accountancy class or be learning the technique of building design and the stress safety levels in a concrete pillar. If being another Mr Teasy-Weasy, Margot Fonteyn or Kevin Keegan takes your fancy, then there are courses on hair care, performing arts and sports management for you, and much, much more. One of the good things about coming to a College for your further

Below: Langley Place in the 1970s.

education is the chance to be away from the school mentality. It does not suit everybody, but there are many others who work better away from the company of much younger children and the more rigid rules of the school. The College offers a more adult treatment and approach, but the responsibility is shifted very much onto the individual. It is very much a case of being up to you. It is the way you respond that will decide your level of success or failure.

Of the four main centres, it is the one at Langley that is easily the most interesting, because of the history it has. The College main building, Langley Hall, became a listed building in 1949. At the time it was the research office for the Ministry of Transport. Its fine 19th century front of red and grey brick led into the main 17th century house. Its three storeys, with their fluted raised stone keys, parapet and delightful mullions and transoms, made this a wonderful place to be an office worker. Later generations of office workers for the Wilkinson Sword Company would find their way to Langley Hall. It was almost a pleasure to have to come to work in such lovely surroundings. During the second world war, RAF personnel had billets here. Officers of the Women's Auxiliary Air Force were given quarters at the Hall. How they would have enjoyed seeing their comrades in the air through the 300 year old windows. Perhaps its most famous use, within the living memory of those of us who are drawing our pensions, was when it was an orphanage in the first part of the 20th century. An orphanage may not sound like the happiest of places or somewhere that would have the best of times, but this was one with a difference.

Firstly, we must go back to the late 19th century. Kittie Carson was an actress who was well known to Victorian audiences. 'Don't put your daughter on the stage, Mrs Worthington'. It always was a precarious occupation. For every star there were ten others

Above left: *Nursing training circa 1917.*
Top: *The development of a new office building behind the original Langley Hall, 1978.*

'resting' and another ten who were destitute. It was in this climate that Kittie and some of her acting friends set up the Actors' Orphanage in Croydon. Its very first President was, perhaps, the most famous actor of his day, Sir Henry Irving. It was 1896 and the days of the workhouse were still very much in evidence. Children who had lost their parents, or whose parents could not support them, had little alternative but to seek the slavery of the workhouse, unless a kind or generous relative could help out. That only happened in books by Dickens or the plays in which Kittie and her chums appeared. In reality, there was no real alternative. The Actors' Orphanage gave some hope. It was set up for the purpose suggested by its name. The children of colleagues who, through death or a combination of poverty or demanding schedules, could no longer care for them, were welcomed. There were, in fact, two homes established, one for boys and one for girls. The Victorian moral code demanded that boys and girls were to be segregated. Remember the Boys' Entrance and Girls' Entrance signs on all our schools that dated from those days?

The orphanage moved several times before settling in Slough. It was 1915 and many actors had been

> *The Actors' Orphanage was set up for the purpose suggested by its name*

sent to the front, never to return. Those who stayed behind found little work and the need for the Actors' Orphanage became even more pressing. But, happily, it was so different from the doom laden types of place that reading Oliver Twist prepares us for. It was a real home, not an institution. The wisteria covered Hall and its lawns echoed to the happy shouts of children, not their miserable pleading for more gruel. As befits the offspring of actors, there would be plays to be performed. Villagers used to flock to see them. So popular were the children, that a sanatorium was added to the Hall by public subscription. Cricket matches against schools and clubs meant that the world outside was visited and children brought to the Hall so that they could see that there was nothing weird about being an orphan. The boys were no fools with the leather and willow. One of the first games played at Langley Hall was against the City of London Second Eleven. An innings victory was a real feather in the cap for the orphanage. The girls played open air sports, but were also encouraged to follow 'useful' pursuits, such as clerical work. It was the attitude of people like one of its most famous

Above: A 1920s sports day.

patrons and Presidents, Gerald du Maurier, that helped it be such a fulfilling place. He always said that the work of the orphanage and its children were what was important, not the self-importance of the people who supported it. Support there was a-plenty. Between the wars, visitors included Gracie Fields, Evelyn Laye, Fay Compton and many more. Autograph hunters would have had a field day. In 1934, Noel Coward became the orphanage's

President and he was followed by Lawrence (Lord) Olivier, by which time the connection with Langley Hall had ended. After 23 happy years the orphanage moved to Silverlands at Chertsey, Surrey. Sir Noel arranged for the children to be evacuated to America for the duration of the war. When peacetime returned, Silverlands re-opened. The orphanage's final move was to Watford, where it ran until 1960. Now known as the Actors' Charitable Trust, the orphanage fund supports Denville Hall, a home for retired actors and actresses. The latest in the line of Presidents is Richard (Lord) Attenborough.

A centenary reunion was held at Langley Hall in 1996, attended by many modern stars and 'luvvies', including Simon Williams, Nicola Pagett, Nicky Henson and Julia Foster. Many of the East Berkshire College performing arts students looked at them and thought, 'I'll be there with you, one day'. Then, those will be the happiest days of our lives.

Left: Langley Actors Orphanage Cricket Team outside a pavilion, 1928. Below: Langley Place as it appeared between 1895 and 1910.

In time with deliveries, in Tune with its customers' needs

Tunes' premises on the Slough Trading Estate would seem more than a little deserted today, with a directorate of just three, of whom two were part-timers, and an office boy; but that is all the workforce consisted of when this firm began to operate from the new Industrial Estate on Ipswich Road, Slough, 60 years ago.

Mr B C Tune, whose background lay in engineering, founded the company on 6th May, 1939, with the idea of supplying engineering consumables to local manufacturers; and, having registered his new company, Bernard Tune invited two friends Stanley Harbord and Albert Knights to join him - which they did, although initially they kept their old jobs on as well - and the three men duly opened up for business at number 510, Ipswich Road.

In those days the large wholesale houses used to make deliveries to Slough once every six or eight weeks at most. Tunes set out to offer a better service. This they did by the simple expedient of taking orders from customers, then going up to London two or three times a week, collecting the items which had been ordered and bringing them back to Slough.

This may sound quite a leisurely way of doing business, but in fact it was no such thing, as it involved catching the 6.30 am train from Slough, getting back to Slough by around midday, and then setting off to deliver the goods to customers on the Company bicycle. Tunes' service was greatly appreciated by the increasing number of manufacturing concerns which were establishing themselves in Slough at that time. But the new distribution company had been in business for barely four months when war changed everything. Mr Harbord volunteered for service (this was unusual as he was both over-age and in a reserved occupation). Tools and materials became increasingly difficult to get hold of, and British industry braced itself and swung round to focus on the war effort. Bernard Tune and Albert Knights, assisted by a couple of men who were over the age for military service, worked day and night and somehow managed to keep the business going until the war was over; and their efforts did not go unrecognised. A cheque arrived from the War Office, and with true patriotic spirit they chose to display it in the reception area rather

Above: *Mr B C Tune, company founder.*
Below: *Tunes trade counter in 1948.*

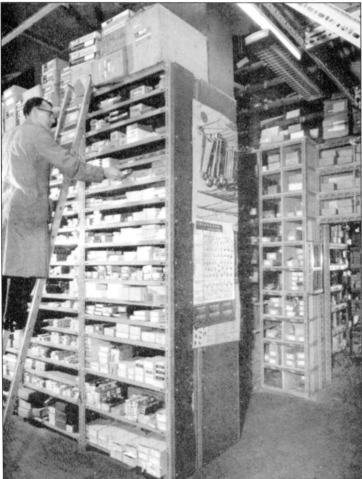

than redeem it through the bank. Visitors to the company today are often quite lost for words as they gaze at the framed cheque made out to Tunes by the Army Pay Office, for the sum of threepence. However, although the company's cashflow situation was healthy enough for them to survive without cashing in this particular cheque, shortage of supplies continued to be a problem for quite a while, and it was not until the 50s that the firm of Tunes really began to take shape.

The firm's efforts during the war had not gone unnoticed, and there was a gratifying demand for their services. With British industry beginning to get back onto its feet after the war years, Tunes established contact with the leading British manufacturers. Expansion commenced, taking the visible form of a number of Nissen-style huts on its existing site. Sadly, Albert Knights died in 1956, and so only saw the company of which he was a co-founder taking the first steps towards fulfilling its potential. Throughout the 60s Tunes continued to grow, stocking an expanding range of products, employing more and more staff, building up a transport fleet, and forging good business relationships with both suppliers and customers. From the outset, the directors had insti-gated a policy of always 'playing fair' with their customers, and the company has never deviated from this. As the business grew and faced new challenges, a more professional approach had to be adopted and

Top: *Delivery vehicles circa 1960.* ***Left:*** *Part of the extensive storage facilities in the early 1960s.*

new methods and systems had to be introduced to improve efficiency, but service to the customer remained of prime importance. The company's slogan 'Tunes for Service' and its commitment to delivering service with speed, competence and courtesy have remained constant factors throughout every stage of its development.

By the mid 70s Tunes, with Bernard Tune as Chairman and Mr Harbord as Managing Director, were employing around 70 people - including Stanley Harbord's son Christopher - and thousands of essential items were stocked in the 14,000 or so square feet provided by their array of Nissen huts. With everything from a door mat to a micrometer, or a broom to an electric drill, while their range of taps and dies was as big as any in the country, the firm was widely known as a major supplier to local industry, with a well-deserved reputation for efficiency and excellent service. Customers and suppliers alike found Tunes a reliable, friendly and completely satisfactory company to deal with; the very first products supplied by Tunes in their early days included, for instance, twist drills and engineers' cutting tools from Dormer Tools and washed, coloured wiping rags from Reliance-Fernhill, and 40 years later both these firms were still proud of their continuing association with Tunes. Following the death of Bernard Tune in 1973, Stanley

Harbord took over as Chairman, and his son Christopher became Managing Director of the firm that was by now established as the largest single engineering distributor in the Thames Valley. Further change lay ahead; within little more than a decade, the company's first computer would be on-line, giving access to accurate and detailed data and revolutionising stock control to such an extent that 30 per cent of existing stock items were identified as being a waste of space and were immediately dispensed with, to be replaced by new lines which within a short space of time were accounting for 40 per cent of orders.

The company celebrated its 50th anniversary in 1989 as a highly-respected and thriving concern, having just recorded an all-time record annual profit. It had been fortunate in being able to take over adjoining sites when the need for further expansion arose, and by 1989 it had spread out in both directions from number 510; stretching from number 506 to number 511 inclusive, it occupied a total floor space of 36,000 square feet. The 18,500 items in stock ranged from workbenches to lathes, milling machines to drilling machines, measuring tools to storage and handling

Above: *Customers at a busy trade counter in the early 1960s.*

with Heather Harbord as joint Managing Director. The number of lines held in stock has risen to 20,000. Each month over 1,000 special orders are processed. That first computer, which Ray Grantham (current Company Secretary) accurately described as having 'tape disks that looked like dustbin lids', has long been superseded; today, some 500 invoices a day are generated, with 24 personnel updating the computer at any one time. Tele-sales is now an important aspect of the business. But the firm's fundamental commitment to customers and staff remains unchanged. Its excellent, long-established relationship with manufacturers means that Tunes can offer customers a substantial range of quality branded goods at extremely competitive prices, while its staff can be relied on to provide quick delivery and well-informed technical advice. Christopher Harbord recently reaffirmed his view that 'The single most important factor . . . is the relationships and trust they (customers) develop with the people inside our business.' The company believes in investing in its staff; it takes training very seriously, and is acknowledged as being one of the leading training companies in the Engineering Industry, with many training awards to its credit. The fact that it has one of the area's lowest staff turnover rates is an indication of a satisfied workforce, composed as it is of a unique blend of youth trainees, enthusiastic management and seasoned experience.

In 60 years this independent, family-owned business has grown from small beginnings into one of the countries' most successful engineering consumable distributors. Customers, staff and suppliers join in wishing the company well as it looks back over its history with pride, and looks forward to the next millennium with every confidence.

Above: The collection counter today. Below: Graham Thomas and the sales team helping to celebrate the firm's 50th anniversary in 1989.

equipment, and welding plant and consumables to janitorial supplies; and non-stock items could be sourced within 24 hours. Tunes' long experience in the trade set it far ahead of its competitors, while the company cleverly managed to adopt radical new technology and progressive ideas without losing its traditional strengths of cautious financial management, good customer relations and a firm reputation for the 'old' values of prompt service, quality and integrity. As a result the staff loyalty which is often found at family-owned firms has always been present to a remarkably high degree at Tunes; the carefully-selected workforce has, at any given time, included a high proportion of long-serving members of staff who have stayed because they enjoy working there.

Ten years further on, Tunes continue to apply the same business principals, and they are still going from strength to strength. Some things have changed; Stanley Harbord retired, and the management team is now headed by Christopher Harbord as Chairman and Managing Director,

Slough Borough Council - doing it their way

Slough Borough Council, in recent history of the area includes not only a period as an 'urban district' (as opposed to a borough), but even more recent transformation into a unitary authority, also there has been a complete switch of location from the county of Buckinghamshire to the county of Berkshire during the - some would say infamous - rearrangement of the local authority boundaries in 1974. Under the new Unitary Status the council intends to grasp every opportunity to make Slough a centre of innovation and excellence. Slough Borough Council remains committed to improving the quality of life for its residents embracing all its duties with enthusiasm and a commitment to equality and progress. The council's five key policy priorities of Social Justice, Economic Development, Community Development, Equality of Opportunity and a Healthy Environment, still remain the firm foundations on which this distinctive, vibrant and proud town is built.

The town Slough can trace its known history back almost a thousand years to Saxon times. From those early days right through into the mid-nineteenth century Slough and its surrounding villages remained largely rural communities, despite the arrival of the famous astronomer Sir William Herschel and his family who became the centre of the Slough social whirl. By the mid-nineteenth century the Great Western Railway had arrived, and of course, progress began in earnest. At the beginning of the twentieth century Slough's population increased dramatically to 11,461 when its boundaries were extended to include parts of neighbouring parishes. It started to be seen as a convenient place to live for those working in London. The first commuters had arrived! As had the first indications of Slough's own commercial possibilities. A site originally owned by the Government at the western end of the town was eventually developed as a trading estate for the company - authorised by an act of parliament - Slough Trading Company, now renamed Slough Trading Estate Ltd. This was Britain's first major trading estate and has made Slough one of the economic success stories of the South-east, with a buoyant economy and many successful companies who help form a trading estate that is Europe's largest in single ownership, companies from Mars to ICI, Ryvita, Citroen, Black & Decker, Calor Gas and Horlicks.

But returning to the here and now... Slough Borough Council operates a full range of the most up-to-date leisure facilities, large, well sited and well maintained historic parks and open spaces, plenty of play areas, a full range of Play and Youth Centres, Libraries, and allotments. Slough's colourful past can be traced at the Museum and through a variety of exciting events throughout the year from the Slough Festival, One World Festival, Slough Canal Festival to the huge Bonfire Spectacular and the Slough Half Marathon now celebrating its 11th year.

Slough's main shopping area, known as the Gold Mile, has undergone some changes over the years to its present day vibrant centre for shopping, eating and entertainment. The now fully pedestrianised central piazza with continental 'Al Fresco' style cafes and bars and the famous

Below: *The Town Hall.*

Centre, the result of a partnership between Slough Borough Council, the Royal Borough of Windsor and Maidenhead and Eton College.

Slough is very much a multi-cultural area, having the first black lady mayor in Europe, in Councillor Lydia Simmons, representing Central Ward. At present over twenty eight per cent of the borough's population are from ethnic minorities; this rises to nearly fifty per cent in the school population. The council is committed to promoting equality, to furthering the town's already strong celebration of cultural diversity, and to maximising the considerable economic success brought to the town by the ethnic minorities.

With its illustrious history, featuring the famous Herschel family; its diverse and complementary sections of population; its many industries, past and present, its commitment to helping all members of the population, whether disabled or able-bodied, to partake equally of council services; and the many other forward looking policies and attributes which Slough, its environs and its council can claim for their own, Slough is primed and ready to take up the challenge of the technological twenty-first century, it is a place where business keeps on growing, where industry is forever changing and expanding and where the careful needs of the people are provided for. It is a town with pride in itself and its achievements. And so it should be!

'Bird Tree' Sculpture providing a focal point for the town square. Now offering a new 'State of the Art' 10 Screen Cinema, lots of lively restaurants and two indoor shopping areas to service Slough and beyond.

Slough has an impressive College of Further Education in Langley and the Thames Valley University with a national reputation for wide ranging professional courses. In May 1999 there was a royal visit in the form of the Duke of Edinburgh touring the new Thames Valley Athletics

Above left: *Queen Elizabeth's visit to the town.*
Top: *High Street in the 1950s.*

Sticking to the very highest standards

To most of us, adhesives mean glue; and glue means something we use when we help the little ones with their Airfix or knock the handle off our favourite mug. In fact, of course, adhesives have a much more fundamental role in everyday life, so fundamental that we barely give it a thought. To name just a few instances: they are an essential part of the packaging around all manner of consumer goods, they fix the laminates onto our furniture, they seal our windows and they are an essential part of bookbinding. Without adhesives, and to be more precise without the special adhesives manufactured by National Starch & Chemical at Slough (part of the ICI group of companies) you would not be turning the pages of this very book, because it was they who supplied the adhesive used in its production. Such a wide range of specialist applications calls for an equally wide range of specialist adhesives and techniques; National Starch & Chemical has a long history of developing innovative new products, and also for working in partnership with the end users, providing a complete technical advisory service and back-up package to ensure optimum performance of their products.

The company was established in Slough in 1927, at premises in Farnham Road. The parent company, the National Gum and Mica Company, had been founded in 1895 in Pennsylvania, USA, by Alexander Alexander, as a manufacturer of gums and sizing for the paper industry. These were the original products of National Adhesives and Resins, as the Slough company was known. Glue manufacture in those days was a very different process from the hi-tec science which it has become - wooden mixing vats and natural starch have been superseded by computer-controlled stainless steel mixing vessels and synthetic polymers, and packaging is now performed by automatic packing lines.

Below: National Starch in the 1930s.
Bottom: *A 1950s view of the premises.*

The company remained at Farnham Road until 1958, when it moved to its present premises; it is now part of the ICI group, who acquired the business from Unilever in 1997. The adhesive industry is very active in research and development work, and the technical team at Slough has consistently come up with quality, high performance, patented products to meet identified needs in the marketplace, and with improved methods of adhesives handling and storage. It has, for instance, developed a carousel system which pre-loads the adhesive blocks into a premelter tank on an industrial machine, thus removing the need for machine operators to manually load the 1Kg blocks. This leads to improved adhesive performance and higher customer productivity. It has developed new adhesives for use with the new range of non-woven textiles, such as the breathable films which promote healthier baby skin; the behaviour of each new material must be studied to find out about shrinkage, ageing, etc, in order to be sure that an adhesive with the correct properties is used. As materials become more and more sophisticated, so must the adhesives.

National Starch's technical team has an extremely broad range of expertise to meet the needs of customers drawn from a cross-section of industry. The needs of the large food companies, for instance, are different from those of the automotive industry; the needs of the bottle-labelling plant are different from those of the bookbinder. In the latter sphere, National Starch & Chemical offers a wide range of quality products based on the complete range of adhesives technology, including a ground-breaking adhesives system know in the trade as COOL-BIND which offers many advantages over other systems because it operates at a lower temperature. As with many adhesive applications, bookbinding may at first sight seem a simple operation, but after a closer study of what is involved it no longer seems quite so simple. Pages which are continually being turned over must have good 'pull strengths'. Some papers, for instance those with heavy, high-gloss coatings - like this page - can be very difficult to bond. And because paper contains moisture, the heat used during the binding process can cause wrinkling. National Starch & Chemical has made it its business to study these and other technical aspects in great detail, and can advise its customers on the most appropriate technology for each application. The same is true of each industry; whether it is dealing with the multinationals or smaller independent companies, National Starch does not simply sell glue but provides a complete service based on a thorough understanding of the customers' needs.

So when it's your grandchildren's turn to show their own kids what Slough used to look like in the previous millennium, 'Memories of Slough' should be in just as good a condition as ever - and National Starch will still be sticking to the same high standards!

Above left: *The interior.*
Top: *Today's employees.*

The Slough company that has built most things - including a good reputation

Geo Streamer Limited was established in Slough at the end of the second world war. In 1994, the year before its 50th anniversary, it became the first building company in Slough to be designated a Chartered Building Company. In order to achieve this status, a firm must be run by qualified professionals who are dedicated to bringing a co-operative approach to all projects and achieving even higher standards of excellence. Geo Streamer Limited certainly meets all these criteria; it has a well-established reputation within the industry for high-quality work, which it ensures by close supervision at every stage, and for its ability to complete on time and within the budgeted cost forecast.

So it may come as surprise to learn that Geo Streamer Limited, which today has a multi-million pound turnover, started on a very small scale indeed. In 1945 George Streamer acquired what was left of a decorating and building contracting business in Ledgers Road, Slough. This once-thriving concern had dwindled away during the war years, and George's ambitious plans to build up a profitable business out of a terraced house, a back yard, a miscellaneous collection building materials and two young lads who were the only employees must have seemed to some a little over-optimistic, to say the least.

With the tireless support of his wife Rose, George Streamer set to work on fulfilling his ambition, providing decorating services and specialist joinery, and carrying out building maintenance and repairs. So successful was he that that by 1971, shortly after its 25th anniversary, the firm was

preparing to move to its current site in White Hart Road, Chalvey, where it had built a headquarters complex of more than 2,000 square yards, comprising a purpose-built workshop, yard and offices.

A number of factors had contributed to the early success of the company. One was the hard work, skill and enthusiasm of the founder which continually drove the company forward, to become the largest local maintenance contractor and joiners. Another was his wife's legendary devotion to duty, typing until all hours of the night and rarely taking time off; and a third was George's readiness to adapt his

Below: *Refurbishment works at a local public house.*
Bottom: *One of the company's earlier lorries leaving the yard.*

owner; Malcolm Mackenzie, a Fellow of the Institute of Builders and ex-Managing Director and Regional Chairman of a public building company, is a far-sighted businessman and a man of tremendous professional ability. Under his guidance, Streamer Building Contractors went on to undertake many major contracts in the local area, including specialist electrical and heating contracts; in 1985 it undertook the design and construction of the new offices in Crendon Street, High Wycombe, for leading estate agents Raffety Buckland, and has carried out contracts for well-known national organisations such as the Nationwide Building Society, Ind Coope, and Horlicks Pharmaceuticals, for whom it constructed new laboratories. Mackenzie Developments was added to the group in 1979, and has built and sold over 100 prestigious houses since that date.

The continued growth and success of this solidly-based company are a tribute both to the man who founded it and built it up into a sound family business, and especially to its current Chairman Malcolm Mackenzie who took it from there to the position of strength which it now occupies. They are also a tribute to the efforts of its loyal workforce, who have worked on everything from churches to public houses, barracks to hotels, offices to old people's homes, council housing to hospitals, and factories to doctors' surgeries. The achievements of Geo Streamer Limited over its first half-century and more, together with its associate company Mackenzie Developments Limited, can be seen in the form of all types of construction within a 30 mile radius of Slough; and the next millennium will bring us many more examples of this outstanding company's fine work.

services to the demands of his customers. Over the years householders have changed their habits with regard to decorating and fitting out their homes, and the nature of Streamer's business diversified accordingly. In the early 70s, by which time Geo Streamer had become virtually a household name as a building and decorating business, George recognised that the modern trend towards 'do-it-yourself' was going to represent a significant sector of the market in future years. So the new White Hart Road site included a sales counter to cater for both trade and public, with special provision for the DIY enthusiasts. Meanwhile contracting remained an important aspect of the business; the new complex included workshops, carpenters' shop, paint stores and glass-cutting equipment, as well as three offices. By now George and Rose Streamer's daughter Rosemary had joined the business, and Rose, the Company Secretary, was gradually delegating the book-keeping and clerical work to her daughter.

Geo Streamer was run as a family business for a total of 30 years, and in that time it expanded from a tiny, virtually unknown firm into a thriving concern with an excellent reputation, operating out of large, modern, purpose-built premises. In 1975 the decision was taken to sell, and a new era began. The business was extremely fortunate in its new

Top: *The company offices and yard.*
Above: *Glazing department.*
Below: *Trade sales counter.*

Delivering great performance

If any readers happen to be the proud owners of a classic Saab 96 two-stroke, and particularly if they are lucky enough to have had it from new, then it's a safe bet that they bought it from Haymill Saab. Founded by George Bate in 1960 and operating from modest premises on the Slough Industrial Estate, Haymill became the original importer for the Saab range of vehicles in the UK, which at the time began and ended with the Saab 96 two-stroke.

Within a few months the Saab Scania group, recognising the importance of the British market, had formed their own subsidiary company, SAAB (GB) Limited, and Haymill Motors immediately became part of the original Saab distribution network, establishing itself as the leading Saab distributor in the UK. During the period which followed Haymill was responsible for the sales and service of Saab cars through some 30 Saab dealerships, stretching across 11 counties.

In 1967 Haymill moved to its present site at Beaconsfield Road, Farnham Common, where it set up new sales, service and parts departments, as well as a petrol station; readers may well remember stopping off there to 'put a Tiger in their tanks' and buy confectionery and accessories from the well-stocked forecourt shop.

In 1978 Saab (GB) Limited adopted a single tier form of operation in the UK and took over control of Haymill. That year the company became the country's leading Saab dealer, with sales of new cars reaching around 150. That year, too, the Fiat franchise was acquired to run alongside Saab, thus augmenting the range of cars available.

The following year Saab (GB) appointed Paul Whitehouse as Dealer Principal to head the team at Haymill Motors. The business gradually grew with the increasing popularity of Saab cars among the British motoring public. The sales team's job was made no easier by three-month delivery delay on new Saabs from Sweden; it was often necessary to negotiate exchanges of stock between dealers in order to supply customers promptly with the car of their choice. However, by 1986 new Saab sales at Haymill had risen to around 400 a year, and the decision was made to relinquish the Fiat franchise and focus exclusively on Saab, which clearly had a bright future ahead of it in this country. At this point the name of the Company was changed to Saab Haymill Limited to reflect the company's new focus on the marque.

Below: *The premises in the 1970s.*
Bottom: *The premises as bought in 1967.*

Following the reorganisation in 1979, the management team remained unchanged until 1992. In that year General Motors seized a golden opportunity to become involved with a quality product and purchased 50 per cent of Saab Automobiles AB. General Motors then approached Paul Whitehouse and the management team at Haymill to propose terms for a management buyout. The team jumped at the opportunity, and now, seven years on, the same management team is controlling the largest private Saab dealership in the UK.

The name of the Company was changed once again, this time to Haymill Saab, to comply with a request from Sweden during the management buyout; and this is the name under which it trades today. In addition to handling around 600 new car sales annually, the company has also established an excellent record for service and parts; these two operations have been so successful that they are now the largest in the country and supply customers worldwide. The Company currently employs over 50 staff and is recognised as one of the most successful Saab dealerships in the world. Many of the staff have been with the Company for over 20 years and have a wealth of knowledge, not only of the latest models in the range - including the superb Saab 9-3 and 9-5 - but also the original 96 two-stroke for which parts are still held in stock . . . of course, if you own one, you'll know that already!

Above left: Haymill Saab today.
Top: The staff in the 1970s.

With Saab firmly established at the fore of the performance car class, its sporting image was reinforced in 1987 when the Company entered into a major sponsorship deal with the successful Oasis Squash Club in Marlow. Readers may remember that Susan Devoy, at that time rated the women's world number one, was based at the Oasis Club, while Sarah Spacey, then the country's top under-14 player, was coached by Bryce Taylor of the Oasis. Saab Haymill added its own sponsorship to that of the parent company Saab (GB), supplying an additional Saab 900 Turbo for the use of Susan Devoy - who went on to win the British Open Championship for the fifth year running and retain her Ladies' World Champion title - and financing a series of matches at the Club. In return, a number of Saab Haymill's clients enjoyed the unique and unforgettable experience of attending coaching clinics held by Susan Devoy and Bryce Taylor.

The company that hands out only the best treatment

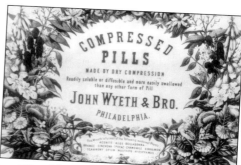

Tucked away in an attractive 14-acres site in Huntercombe Lane South, off the Bath Road, lies the UK Headquarters of Wyeth Laboratories, the fastest growing prescription medicine company in the UK, manufacturer of the UK's leading Infant Formula and one of the world's foremost healthcare corporations.

Wyeth Laboratories came to Slough in 1962; but to trace the origins of the business we must go back more than a century and a quarter, and half way round the globe. The Company was founded in Pennsylvania, America in 1834, when two young pharmacists, John and Frank Wyeth, started to look at ways to make medicines more palatable, and also at methods of compounding drugs to form tablets, which could then be put into large-scale production. By 1862 their research had borne fruit. A manufacturing system had been developed, and a range of Wyeth treatments was available for wholesale distribution; and the outbreak of the American Civil War opened up a quite unforeseen market for products of this nature. Throughout the war Wyeth supplied medicines to the Union Army, in such quantities that the fortunes of the Company rose significantly.

Following a fire which destroyed their original premises, the Company re-established itself on a new site, where it expanded from tablet production into other hitherto unknown forms of medicine. Maintaining the innovative tradition of its founders, it made the first glycerine suppositories, effervescent salts and soluble gelatine capsules ever produced in America; and any readers who are planning a trip to Washington in the near future might be interested to know that the Smithsonian Institute houses the first rotary table press, developed by Wyeth.

In 1907 John Wyeth died and his son Stuart succeeded him. By this time Wyeth's products had become well established outside America; they had been available in the UK since 1878, where they were handled by Silas Burrough, of Burrough Wellcome fame. It was Stuart Wyeth who foresaw the future benefits of overseas expansion, and in 1924, five years before his death, he set up manufacturing facilities in England. From here, exports were sent all over the Commonwealth - Australia, New Zealand and India - and to South Africa, and other distant continents.

Following Stuart Wyeth's death in 1929, his interest in the Company passed, under the provision of his Will, to Harvard University. As ownership of a growing international pharmaceutical company lay somewhat outside its normal sphere of activity, the University sold it to American Home Products (AHP) for $1.8 million. AHP, with current assets of $21 billion, is still the parent company today.

By 1943 the Company had bought a number of other pharmaceutical businesses. The acquisition of the SMA Corporation was of particular significance as it brought Wyeth into a completely new sphere of activity. SMA had been involved in the development of baby formula since 1918 and had become a household name; following the takeover, Wyeth was able to enter this market at a high level, and it is now a major world supplier of baby formula.

Top Left: *John Wyeth, founder of the company.*
Top Right: *Early product label.*
Above: *One of the earliest Wyeth innovations was the rotary tablet press, developed by the company in 1882.*

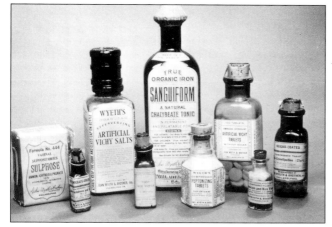

The company's continued success over the years is a direct result of its commitment to research, and its ability to apply the latest developments in medical science and develop an effective range of products to meet the current needs of the population. For instance, during World War II the Company's entire manufacturing schedule was adjusted to War Department needs. The Company was a pioneer in commercial penicillin production, and in 1944 was supplying 60 per cent of world demand for penicillin. It also focused on the development of vaccines, introducing vaccines for smallpox, cholera, rabies, influenza and diphtheria. Today the Company is established as one of the world's leading vaccine producers, and no doubt many readers, in going for their annual 'flu jab, are benefiting in very practical terms from research

Above: *Some of Wyeth's early pharmaceutical specialities.*
Right and Below: *Wyeth research laboratory with Penicillin deep fermentation tanks in background.*

carryied out at Wyeth. The Company's vaccines to combat respiratory infections are also very widely used, and this year the first once-only dose meningitis C vaccine became available - developed by Wyeth.

A great deal of medical progress was made in the course of the 50s, 60s, 70s and 80s, and during this period the Company's Research and Development team went on to develop many new products, introducing into the UK treatments for conditions as varied as mental illness, infectious diseases and gastro-intestinal conditions. And it was as a result of this marked increase in the number of products that Wyeth moved to Slough. Up until 1962 the Company had operated from a number of locations in and around London, latterly in Euston Road; however, as business increased, more manufacturing space became a priority, closely followed by the need for more office accommodation. So in 1957 production was moved to a new site at Havant, Hampshire, which still remains a major production

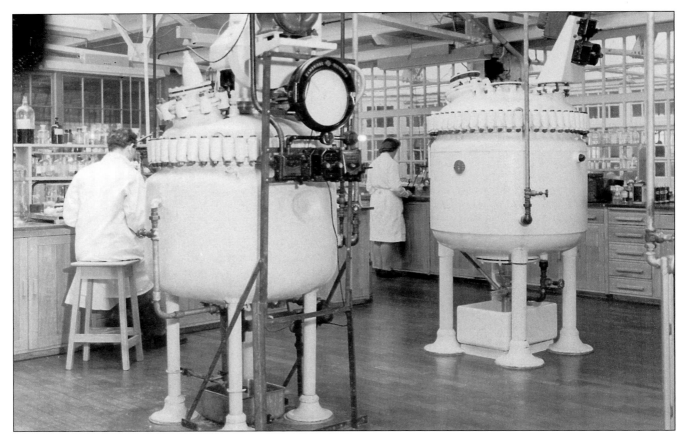

who make Anadin, Centrum and Advil, and a contingent of European Headquarters staff, while the company has an additional site in Slough at 392 Bath Road.

In all, Wyeth employs some 1500 people in the UK with a further 1500 in two production sites in the Republic of Ireland. The Company is currently the fourth largest supplier of medicine to the NHS with key treatment for cardiovascular disease, cancer and mental disorders and supplies anti-inflammatory, anti-infection and gastro-enterology drugs, contraception, hormone replacement therapy and vaccines, in addition to its SMA Baby Food range. It has recently introduced a new drug for haemophilia and will shortly be launching a range of new vaccines, and new treatments for arthritis and to assist in transplant surgery. With its parent company currently spending £1.5 billion a year on research into new medicines, Wyeth's positive impact on world health in the future is likely to be even more significant than in the past. And the Company's future will be shared with

Slough; while its association with the town began only 37 years ago, it has proved a happy one, and Wyeth looks forward to making a contribution to the story of Slough through their medical developments in the years ahead.

centre today. Then in 1962 a new Headquarters building was constructed in Slough. These premises, with their subsequent additions, now form the centre of Wyeth's UK operation, also housing its sister company Whitehall

Top: *Penicillin deep fermentation vessels.*
Right: *Over a century of pioneering developments in pharmaceuticals.*

Shopping that goes from from strength to strength

It took an incredible 1,050,000 bricks, 76,930 tonnes of concrete and 3,500 tonnes of steel reinforcements to build Slough's state-of-the-art Observatory Shopping Centre, which opened in July 1991 in response to Slough's rapidly expanding population. When work began on the new centre, few could have visualised the eventual outcome - a lively, bustling facility with a total of 185,000 square feet of climatically controlled shopping area, and a brightly lit parking space on two levels for more than 800 vehicles.

The inspiration for the Centre's name came from the famous astronomer Sir William Herschel, who made his home in Slough back in 1786. A builder of powerful telescopes, Herschel discovered Uranus in March 1781 - a discovery which brought him instant fame and official recognition as 'King's Astronomer' to King George III.

Shoppers were immediately at ease with the town's new complex. The idea of browsing in a comfortable facility that was under cover and therefore sheltered from cold winds and driving rain held great appeal. The temperature-controlled environment, warm and snug in the howling winds of winter was also a cool refuge from the hot summer sun.

As well as the huge number of shops of every kind, including the big high street names such as Woolworths, Argos, Top Shop and Top Man, the centre offers the benefits of other key services such as the HFC Bank, the Abbey National Building Society, a post office - and even a leisure and fitness centre.

There is little need for shoppers to go elsewhere, as linked by the malls almost 50 shops and stores ensure that most if not all of their needs can be supplied under one roof, from sportswear to software and from stationery to jewellery. And when shoppers have 'shopped till they dropped' they can take their weary feet into the Cafe Giardino to enjoy a substantial meal or to simply order a steaming cappuccino and sit and watch the world go by.

In the years that have passed since the opening of the Observatory, the shopping centre has gone from strength to strength, and the quality of tenants is being continually upgraded. Such a development, of course, does not stand still for long, and whatever developments are in the wind, the shoppers of Slough are sure to remain happy with the shopping centre that has served them well from the day of its opening.

Above and below: *The Observatory Shopping Centre.*

Half a pound of treacle...

Few people who remember the old rhyme are aware that delicious Golden Syrup was invented by Charles Eastick as long ago as 1884. He and his brother John Joseph were employed as chemists by Abram Lyle & Sons Ltd, one of around 150 sugar refiners in Britain at the time.

The two brothers left Lyle's in 1890, John to oversee the Bundaberg sugar plantations in Australia and Charles to run production at Martineaus Sugar Refinery at Whitechapel - thereby establishing something of a family tradition as his eldest son Fredrick and eldest grandson Bernard also pursued successful careers at Martineaus, with Fredrick becoming joint Managing Director and Bernard, Production Director.

During the 1920s small amounts of specialised sugars were being imported to Britain as it was not economic for the larger refineries to manufacture these. In 1928 Charles established a specialist factory on the then new Slough Industrial Estate to produce those sugars, using raw materials from Martineaus as well as cut candied peel and fruit drink cordials made from oranges and lemons. The company - Fruit Products Limited, with the brand Ragus® (sugar inverted) - is the longest established company on the estate, having been situated there from the very outset, on the site which it still occupies today - 193 Bedford Avenue. Charles ran Fruit Products Limited alongside his work at the Martineaus Refinery and was joined at Slough by his youngest son Douglas. Here the product range remained virtually unchanged until the second world war, when shortage of fruit caused the production of fruit drinks to be abandoned. Charles was also made responsible for administering the UK wartime sugar rationing quotas, for which he was awarded an MBE.

By 1937 the company was known simply as Ragus Products, the industry seeing more and more companies merging, by 1957 there were 21. At this time the confectioner/food manufacturer still had a wide choice of supplier, but 20 years later, with strikes affecting the British sugar industry, just three

Above right: *An early golden syrup lid.*
Above left: *Charles Eastick, founder of the company.*
Below: *A 1970s delivery tanker.*

is employed in testing of the breakdown of sugars, using HPLC meters.

Potential growth areas for the company are GMO Free and Organic sugars and syrup. Main customers for Ragus' range of dry and liquid sugars include the baking and brewing industries, chilled and frozen foods, confectionery, breakfast cereals, sauces, preserves and soft drinks manufacturers. In addition to its wide range of standard products the company produces a diverse range of specialist products made to exact specifications and packed either in standard packaging or, again to customers' own specification. With a production facility designed to work to short lead times, Ragus has a well earned reputation for being very responsive to customers' needs. It also has a reputation for being a friendly place to work, with many long serving employees who have served under successive generations of the founder's family and likewise whose own fathers and sons have worked there.

There are few firms today which have achieved such success without sacrificing their independence, and few families that have such an unbroken history and dedication to a single product.

manufacturers remained. The majority had been taken over by the amalgamated company of Henry Tate & Abram Lyle. Ragus was the only private company; it celebrated its Golden Jubilee under the proud slogan: 1928-1978 and still independent! It still holds this unique position today, 71 years since it was founded. Succession passed first to Douglas, then to Charles Eastick's youngest grandsons Ronald, who ran production and Barrington, who ran sales. Since 1990 the company has been run by Charles' youngest great grandsons, Peter who runs production, James and Benjamin who run sales and marketing.

The raw materials and equipment in use at Ragus today are essentially the same as those used 71 years ago. The range of raw materials is somewhat wider today, and includes many forms of glucose syrups, caramelised sugar syrups and syrups with the inclusion of flavours, while more advanced technology

Top: Golden syrup filling in the 1970s.
Above left: The offices in the 1970s.
Right: A sales meeting in the millennium.

Slough's own electrical retail wizard

In the years following his National Service Glyn Evans, a trained electrical engineer, aimed at owning his own business. By 1956 he and his wife Gwyneth were ready to open their first electrical shop-cum-ironmongers at 322 High Street, Slough. Although they stocked paraffin, hardware and garden requisites the main line was that of labour saving electrical appliances. Post-war housewives were avid buyers of machines that not only had been out of production for nearly a decade but which to many were a dream fostered by films showing the user-friendly American life-style.

In 1960 Glyn went to the Olympic Games in Rome as the winning guest of the national company for which he had sold the most appliances in a regional competition. He left his wife and new born son at home as young Paul was too young for foreign travel. In both 1962 and 1963 his selling successes won holidays in Bermuda and Miami which he and Gwyneth were able to enjoy thanks to a relative who stepped in to look after the children. Glyn told the Slough

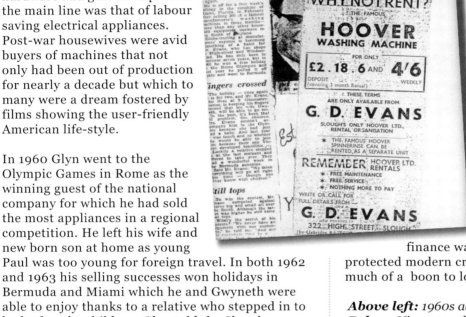

Observer that he'd never had an argument with a customer and that he provided an after sales service second to none.

For all these evident signs of success the early days were not all a bed of roses. Hire Purchase may have enabled customers to buy what they wanted but it did not ensure that the retailer always got paid for his sales. Bad debts and repossessions were costly liabilities to any business even in the 1960s when washing machines could be had for a deposit of under £3 and weekly payments of 4/6d (22.5p). There was no refund made for Purchase Tax paid by defaulting hire purchasers. Many readers will remember Purchase Tax as a simpler one off fore-runner of VAT introduced to finance war debts. The insurance protected modern credit card system has proved as much of a boon to local suppliers as it has to

Above left: *1960s advertising.*
Below: *Vincent and his father on deliveries in 1961.*

purchasers seeking a simpler form of borrowing for immediate purchases.

G D Evans, as an agent for Hoover Ltd Rentals, provided free maintenance and servicing all included in the price! Other famous brands carried in the Evans shops, then and now, are Bendix, Electrolux and Hotpoint. Hard work and a dedication to the principle that the customer, who pays all the bills, must be treated with respect enabled G D Evans to expand. Other shops were opened in Windsor Road and at numbers 333 and 331 High Street. Eventually the idea of buying separate electrical appliances to ease daily housework gave way to overall plans for fitted kitchens. The principles of work study and ergonomics led to the clean uncluttered look accepted as normal today.

The Evans family, and their staff who visit customers in their own homes, have over 30 years of expertise in safe fitting of electrical domestic appliances. The goods supplied include not only the mechanical 'maids of all work' that undertake dish and clothes washing while the modern householder is at work or play but hobby appliances also. As yet vacuum cleaners still require supervision by a dedicated

operator, that is the housewife or a Man-Friday. Gardeners in our variable climate can now rely on electrically heated propagators and temperature controlled greenhouse ventilators to ensure that their plants get the best chances in an uncertain life. Like all electrical machinery which operates in conjunction with water these need both skilled installation and maintenance.

It has become so common for kitchens to be equipped with well designed separated ovens and hobs, microwaves and plug-in slow cookers and bread makers that people have all but forgotten what uncomfortable black holes the average kitchens of the 1950s and 60s were. Fridges were rare, freezers and dishwashers unheard of while home launderers considered themselves lucky if they had a top loaded spin drier. Whatever the customers' requirements may be they can rest assured that at G D Evans, now run by Glyn and Gwyneth's son Roger, they will be served with a smile. In the unlikely event of something not working as it should the firm will follow the founder's precept of putting it right without argument.

Above: *A display tent in Agars Plough, in August 1963.*

Professional help is at hand

Harris & Cartwright can trace their roots back to 1922 when Harold Henry Harris set up in practice in Slough High Street. Mr Harris had come to Slough to manage the first world war ammunitions dump which was situated on what is now the Trading Estate. Who could know that in the following years the practice would increase to four offices with over 100 members of staff?

Mr Harris later joined up with Richard Francis Cartwright to form Harris & Cartwright and they operated from Mr Cartwright's home at 14 Bath Road, Slough. As more members of staff joined, the property was extended and became used just as offices.

John Bayford joined the firm as a trainee solicitor in 1960. He can be given much credit for the growth of the partnership and the firm's increasing presence in Slough during the 1970s. John was senior partner of the firm from 1974 until 1989. His brother, Graham, took over the reins at the firm's offices in High Street, Burnham until 1992 when the present Managing Partner, Paul Norris, took over the role. Paul joined the firm in 1979 as a trainee and the firm has continued to grow under his leadership.

In 1986 the firm merged with the local solicitors, Roderic Miles & Co. which operated from 14 High Street, Slough and the practice ran from both offices until 1989 when they consolidated and moved to Windsor Crown House, Windsor Road. Roderic Miles has over 40 years of local experience and is very passionate about Slough and its people. "It's a marvellous place," he says, "it has had virtually full employment for most of its history and has, on average, a higher standard of living than many other towns - in the 1960s it was supposed to be England's second most wealthy town."

So much has changed in law since the old days when each lawyer would do a bit of everything from criminal law to house-buying. Now, young solicitors specialise in a particular field straight away. The firm continued to grow and took additional premises in Church Street for its commercial department in 1996.

In 1997 the firm celebrated its 75th anniversary and marked the occasion by becoming the first legal firm in the Thames Valley and the fourth in the south of England to achieve the national Investors in People Award. This Award is granted to organisations who prove that they meet criteria relating to the development of their staff to best meet their business objectives. Harris & Cartwright

Above left: *Harold Henry Harris.*
Below: *A letterhead from the 1960s.*

TELEPHONE: SLOUGH 20379 (2 LINES)

HARRIS & CARTWRIGHT,
Solicitors
Commissioners for Oaths

R. F. CARTWRIGHT, LL B (LOND).
E. R. MOUTRIE.

OUR REF. JAG/VP

YOUR REF.

14, Bath Road,
Slough, Bucks.

20th February, 1961.

Dear Madam,

We thank you for your letter of the 18th instant and note your application for the vacancy in our offices as a shorthand-typist.

We should like to see you with regard thereto and shall be glad if you will kindly arrange to call at 11.15 on Saturday morning this week the 25th instant.

Yours faithfully,

Court in Henley. More than 100 members of the firm gathered in 1920s fancy dress for a night of revelry, food and wine.

About 10 years ago the firm also started acting for the RAC. The Personal Injury Department acts for RAC members who are involved in road traffic accidents in Berkshire, Buckinghamshire and Middlesex. In addition the firm now acts in respect of the RAC's own vehicle fleet, including Patrol and Reflex recovery vehicles as well as all staff cars for the whole of the Country south of Birmingham. The firm made national news in December 1998, when it obtained record damages of £9.2 million for one of its clients who was involved in a road traffic accident. This was a very complex case which was heard in the High Court over seven weeks. The damages were high due to the particular circumstances of the case and to take into account the high anticipated earnings that the client would have received if the accident had not occurred.

can boast that amongst its staff there is a marathon runner and some parachute jumpers. In August 1997 a team of six solicitors jumped 2,500 ft at Hinton-in-the-Hedges airfield to raise £7,500 for local charity The Slough Foyer, whose aim is to help the many hundreds of homeless and unemployed young people to break out of the 'no job, no home' vicious circle. As a firm, Harris & Cartwright recognise the need to support the local community.

In May 1998 the Partners hosted a major beanfeast for past and present employees at the prestigious Phyllis

Above left: *Part of the company's 75th anniversary celebrations in May 1998. The partners and staff dressed in 1920s costume. From left to right: Dan Walters, Stephen Fuller, Paul Norris, Mark Moorcroft, Chris Gooderidge, Kent Pattinson.*
Top: *The company's premises in Windsor Road.*
Right: *Richard Francis Cartwright.*

In 1999, Harris & Cartwright achieved another first in Slough by setting up its own Financial Services Department.

Bath Road - where life is more varied than a Soap

Number 225 Bath Road, Slough has been a Sara Lee business site since 1958. During its early years its best known product was Aspro tablets, which the Australian parent company had been manufacturing since 1915. By the time work commenced on developing the site on the Bath Road, however, its pharmaceutical production had begun to diversify, and further expansion was anticipated. Accordingly, the new Slough factory was designed to accommodate expansion of up to 100 per cent over the next few years. It was built with a single warehouse and a single production area, and equipped with modern 'U-flow' production lines. One of them was a dedicated 'Aspro' line to facilitate unimpeded, one-level flow from raw material to finished product, with a minimum of human handling. The plant was virtually the first British example of the 'windowless factory', relying on artificial light and ventilation - a concept which had already been tried and proved successful in other parts of the world. Careful planning went into every aspect of the design and construction of the Slough factory. Staff welfare was one of the organisation's highest priorities, and the objective was to create a good place to work in, both physically and psychologically. The whole site deservedly met with enthusiastic approval from the architectural critics of the time. Planned to combine convenience with flexibility, and decorated in a contemporary style using aluminium and natural wood, textiles, plastics and ceramics, it provided bright, spacious, comfortable staff lounges, canteens, cafeterias and locker rooms, while outside were lawns, courtyards, flowers and fountains. The factory itself covered more than 250,000 square feet and the office area, with over 250 desks, covered almost an acre. Additionally there were executive offices, conference rooms and a reception area. Recognition of the tremendous importance of product research and development was reflected in the provision of a well-equipped research department. Throughout, great attention was paid to detail and everything was furnished and decorated with a view to minimising strain and monotony. Preparation of the site began in 1955; the factory was completed in 1958. The care which had gone into its construction was rewarded by the high output which made an immediate and significant impact on the local community.

Above: Radox Herbal Bath - one of the company's products. Below: Early production lines.

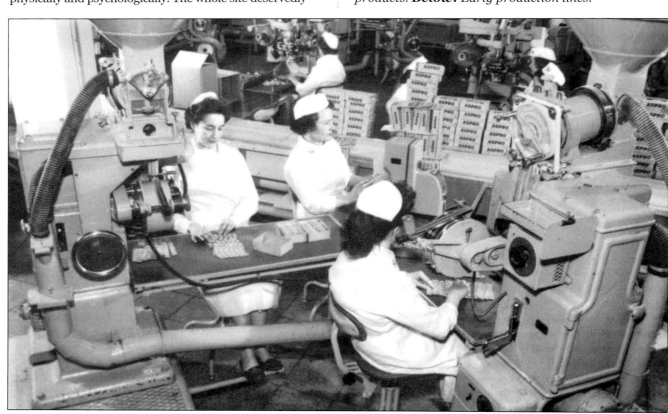

Forty years later, the organisation has moved away from the pharmaceutical industry where it once had its roots. Although the healthcare division was not sold until 1991, the change of direction began very soon after the opening of the Slough factory. A programme of acquisition commenced with the purchase of Fields of Bond Street in 1958, followed by E Griffiths Hughes in 1959, and in 1963 the company acquired the rights to Matey Bubble Bath and Matey Powder - no doubt a very familiar name to many readers! Another big household name joined the list in 1970 with the launch of Radox Liquid, and subsequent years have seen continual expansion of the range of household and body care products produced at Slough. The company has gone from strength to strength, with its current range extending across the shoe care, body care, air freshener, insecticide and speciality sectors, and including famous brands such as Kiwi, Meltonian, Badedas, Ambi-Pur, Vapona and Brylcreem.

Throughout the process of evolution which culminated in the site adopting the name of Sara Lee Household & Body Care in 1997, the fundamental principles upon which the Slough enterprise was founded have changed remarkably little. As part of the giant multinational Sara Lee Corporation, the company is as committed as ever to investment. This covers its workforce, processing and production facilities, and product research, achieving performance excellence through teamwork and innovation. Meanwhile, it has also developed an active role within the local community as a member of the Slough Strategy Group. Readers may know this is a partnership between industry and commerce, education, Slough Borough Council and other voluntary and local organisations that promote local initiatives to improve Slough as a place to live and work. Sara Lee is involved in

a number of local initiatives, including providing managers as mentors for local schoolchildren, advising young people on job interviewing skills, and running a work experience programme for school pupils. The company has also signed up to the Leadership Challenge, which promotes employment opportunities for members of ethnic minorities.

In 1988 the company celebrated 30 successful years on the Bath Road with a Family Day. It marked its 40th anniversary in 1998 with a two-day circus event enjoyed by all the company's employees, their families and friends. Meanwhile the organisation continues to work hard to deliver the best products and services, taking pride in its achievements so far and knowing that the future holds much more success in store.

Above: *Manufacturing in the 1990s.*
Below: *The company premises.*

High quality, hi-tech hydraulic engineering

During the second world war Mr F Tharby, a local garage proprietor and entrepreneur, turned his energies to the war effort. He formed a company which he called Versatex, obtained machines from the USA on a lease-lend basis, and installed them at premises at number 2 Green Lanes, Datchet. There, equipped with capstan lathes, camshaft grinders, drills and mills, and using carbon and forged steels, Versatex commenced production of a range of high precision components; the main machine shop was used by Baker Platinum, to supply contact breakers for aero engines, and by the time the war came to an end Versatex was an established and thriving business. In 1947 Mr Tharby registered the company. That same year the company overcame its first setback when the River Thames flooded throughout Datchet, following a very severe winter.

With war work at an end, Mr Tharby needed to find an alternative activity for his company. Before the war he had been the owner of Leigh Park Motors in Datchet, so, with contacts in the motor trade, he initially moved into engine reconditioning with the company under new ownership and component manufacture continued, primarily for the valve sector. Subsequently, following major investment in extensive, up-to-date production facilities, the company was in a position to broaden its activities to include a wide range of high technology industrial and defence applications. With new equipment including automatic lathes, cylindrical, surface and centreless grinders and boring, milling and broaching machines housed alongside the existing drilling machines, surface finishing and cleaning plant in a total shop floor area of 9,500 square feet, Versatex, with the

benefit of further investment into CNC turning lathes in 1985, was now able to produce most turned components up to 60mm diameter and 150mm chucking, offering prototype, medium batch and long runs, mainly in carbon steel and alloys. It launched an active policy of expansion and diversification, with its progressive management team implementing computer-aided systems to ensure fast quotations, reliable delivery dates and guaranteed high quality.

Versatex's enhanced production capabilities quickly led to it becoming an approved supplier to major companies such as

Below: J&S vertical honing machines.
Bottom: Main machine shop. Single spindle cam automatics.

scratch a substantial and loyal customer base. In later years, along with the rest of Britain's manufacturing industry, it had to find ways to survive the miners' strike of the early 1970s; this it did by operating on a three-day week. Later that decade, cut-throat competition from abroad resulted in a further recession and the need to squeeze down prices and costs in order to stay in business. And more recently, the period between 1989 and 1993 proved to be another extremely difficult time for the company, with the production engineering industry again hit by a severe recession; again Versatex managed to remain solvent and protect the interests of its workforce, while maintaining its commitment to providing its loyal customers with a first-class service.

The firm remained in private ownership until 1967, with proprietor Mr F Tharby assisted for many years by his brother-in-law Tom Jacobs. It was then sold to Gripperods Holdings, and this company was in turn bought out in 1984, by British Land. Three years later a management purchase was negotiated, and Versatex was established in its current form. At the time of writing, the company is currently owned by Mr TD Henson and is contemplating a possible acquisition of another engineering company to complement and expand its resources. Broadly speaking, its future plans are to diversify within its own product range while maintaining the versatility, the quality and the reliability of service upon which its reputation is based.

Smiths Industries, Dowty Hydraulics, and Lucas. Today its customer base includes the major multinational corporations in the hydraulic, pneumatic and defence industries, to whom it supplies high volumes of high precision components produced in sub-assembly stages, ready for the customers' own assembly lines. Versatex can also manufacture a range of items such as hydraulic activators, relief valves and spool valves to clients' own specifications. The emphasis is still on quality; strict quality procedures are observed throughout the manufacturing process, where the aim is for zero defects, and inspection is carried out in a fully-equipped inspection department to ISO 9002 standard.

Throughout its history the company has remained at its original premises in Datchet; the choice of location proved fortunate, with the growth of the motorway network around London working in its favour and bringing it all the advantages of excellent road links with the rest of Britain. In other respects, however, Versatex's fifty-two years of existence have not been without their share of challenges and setbacks. As a young company, it successfully made the transition from war work to sub-contractor to industry, establishing from

Top: *High precision honing and grinding department.*
Above left: *High speed threading and broaching machines.* ***Below:*** *CNC Machining department.*

Fighting fire...in the air!

Fire prevention is a part of life to many servicemen and others in high risk occupations. Captain Hubert Salmond, Royal Indian Navy, retd, watched a motor-racing friend burn to death following a crash from which he might have recovered. This unfortunate accident inspired Salmond to invent an electrical cut off switch for motor cars. He teamed up with Anders Mathisen, a Danish engineer-cum-patents agent and together they marketed their GRAVity INERtia switch which also gave them the name Graviner for their company. Working on the basis that fire prevention could save lives in the air as well as on the ground this device was developed into a complete system. Civil manufacturers said that customers were not prepared to pay extra for safety but the Royal Air Force was.

Co-operation with the RAF in 1938-39 led to an order for 1000 sets of switches and fire extinguishers. Initially these were produced in Salmond's garden shed until the Wilkinson Sword Company agreed to manufacture them in their Acton factory. Following an official directive during World War II, a second factory was established at Poyle Mill, Colnbrook in order to meet increased production demands. Crash operated and turn-over switches initiated extinguishers which put out fires in remote areas of the aircraft while hand operated extinguishers enabled air-crew to attack fires in accessible parts of the airframe.

The post-war run down of the armed forces coincided with the growth of civil aviation from a rare luxury to the common place movement of people and cargo. The company first produced its 'FIREWIRE™' continuous fire detection sensors in the 1950s. This technology was unique to Graviner and FIREWIRE™ is still manufactured today. Parallel to this was the introduction of the Oil Mist Detector (OMD) for monitoring potentially dangerous vapour in marine diesel engines. This product was so successful that, within a decade, 60 percent of the

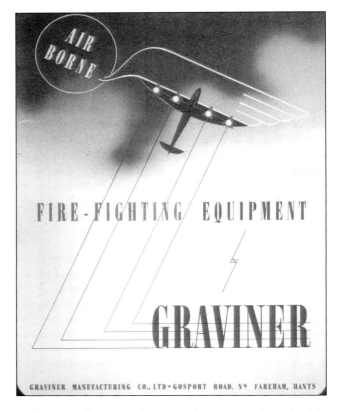

AIR BORNE

FIRE-FIGHTING EQUIPMENT

by

GRAVINER

GRAVINER MANUFACTURING CO., LTD · GOSPORT ROAD, N° FAREHAM, HANTS.

world's merchant marine vessels were equipped with Graviner OMDs. 'Checking the Graviners' became a normal part of safety routine at sea.

Military tank crews on active service would be rejected by most insurance companies. Thanks to Graviner the crews of personnel carriers and main

Top left: *Anders Mathisen, founder of the company.*
Top right: *The cover of a 1930s brochure of the company's products.*

battle tanks could travel more safely even though surrounded with fuel and ammunition. Currently 45,000 tanks around the world are fitted with Graviner fire protection systems. Further research projects led to the development of fire detection and explosion protection in other high risk areas. Civil users of Graviner equipment spread rapidly to include industrial plant, vehicles, trains, mines and off-shore drilling rigs. Companies worldwide invested in Graviner equipment, concluding that prevention was less costly than replacing fire damaged equipment.

The 1980s saw Graviner pass through different owners including Allegheny International Inc, USA and RHP Group plc. The current building was opened by HRH the Duke of Kent in 1985. Four years later Graviner merged with an American fire protection manufacturer called Walter Kidde and became known as Kidde Graviner. As a consequence of further organisational expansion and restructuring Kidde Graviner now concentrates its expertise on fire protection systems for aircraft and military vehicles. Modern developments such as ultra fast optical flame detection and advanced fire extinguishing systems are incorporated into the most reputable and up-to-date civil and military aircraft. In the international field Kidde Graviner has combined with the US based companies Walter Kidde Aerospace, Fenwal Safety Systems, Santa Barbara Dual Spectrum and L'Hotellier of France. This amalgamation of expertise, referred to as Kidde

Aerospace and Defence, provides the world's most comprehensive range of safety equipment to protect lives and equipment from the devastating effects of fire and explosions on the ground and in the air.

Kidde Graviner is a subsidiary of Kidde International which is a major division of Williams PLC, a group that enjoys unrivalled experience and financial stability in the field of dealing with fires and explosions worldwide.

Above and facing page, bottom: *Exhibition stands for the company from the 1950s and 60s.* **Below:** *The impressive premises today.*

Almost as important as power itself

Kopex International Ltd provide flexible conduit and connectors to protect and contain electrical systems. The Kopex pliable tubes were first produced by Kopex Maschinen AG in Zurich, Switzerland in 1937. Imagine the versatility of watertight, pressure resistant tubes and piping which can be bent into shape by hand and cut to length using a sharp knife. Such a facility makes maintenance and replacement easy, fast and economical. Uni-Tubes were set up in England in 1946 at the Old Brewery, Alpha Street, Slough to expand international sales. Sometime later the company opened another factory on Slough Trading Estate. In 1950 S. Smith & Sons Ltd gained a 51 percent interest in Uni-Tubes to enhance their car heater division.

Kopex Pliable conduits and connectors are used in a wide variety of industrial and transport situations. They protect electrical wiring from damage by pressure, bending and the corrosive action of chemicals and natural elements. Lloyds Register of Shipping, the oil industry and the RNLI recognise the high quality of Kopex used in in-ship wiring. The demands made on protective conduit in the stressful conditions of the aviation, mining and military fields are met equally well by Kopex products. The ability of Kopex Pliable to survive knocks and vibration, dust and great temperature changes is essential to the survival of personnel working in such extreme conditions. The three standard types are made of layers of bitumen infused paper, except in the heavy duty mode, lead coated steel or aluminium inners and a PVC outer. Add to this four Specialist variations which can handle temperature extremes ranging from 40 degrees C below freezing to 150 degrees C of heat.

Ten years later Uni-Tubes pioneered PTFE Tubing for use in Fliteline conduits and high pressure hoses. Whereever

hydraulic tubes are used, in the retractable landing gear of aircraft, food processing plants and other liquid movement situations Kopex tubes are used as they are in all areas where electric wiring circuits need protection from stress and corrosion.

In 1963 Uni-Tubes became a full part of Smiths Industries whose products included heat and acid proof flue linings for chimneys. The Portland Plastics division specialised in Portex medical tubing for a wide spectrum of use in operating theatres, wards and laboratories. In 1967 the company moved all of its sites to 189 Bath Road, Slough where they were to stay for the next 30 years. On a more prosaic scale the development of DIY home plumbing during the 1970s fostered the sales of Kopex Copperbend, a hand bendable flexible copper piping ideal for use by the home handyman.

Above: *An early brochure showing some of the applications for the company's product - electrical conduit systems.* ***Below:*** *The reception in the late 1960s.*

The 1980s saw a change from metallic conduits to recent developments in new flexible stress and corrosion resistant nylon tubing. This was followed in 1983 by the identification of the market for chemical smoke and fume resistant conduit which Kopex produced with explosion proof barrier glands. In 1986 Uni-Tubes became Kopex International Ltd and the next year the firm produced, and patented, its own unique copper cutting tool called Pipeslice. This became a best seller throughout the plumbing service industries.

The Kopex Flexible Metallic Conduits and Connectors are capable of bending, twisting and springing back into shape despite constant movement and hostile climatic and working conditions. These tough tubes are equally at home in Arctic ice breakers, High Speed trains and the demanding petro-chemical industries throughout the world. The Liquid Tight models have a layer of string or copper wire packing around the core of galvanised steel which is protected by an outer layer of PVC. The latter can be oil resistant and, like all Kopex conduit, meets standards set by Lloyds, Det Norske Veritas, Canadian Standards Association, the Underwriters Laboratory and NEMKO.

In 1990 Kopex ceased production of flue linings and Copperbend products as a result of competitive pricing in an area where the cost of the raw material was reaching for the sky. However the range of connectors, lock nuts and adaptors etc in brass, stainless steel and nylon continues to meet the stringent needs of all who rely on Kopex tubing.

In 1997 the Bath Road site was redeveloped, and became a retail park with Kopex moving to 675 Ajax Avenue on the Trading Estate.

Kopex clients are served by an unrivalled research and development department backed by a world wide sales and service team. Together they ensure that new industries receive the same innovative standard of product as established clients who benefit from upgraded conduit designed for the world's most demanding circumstances.

Top: *British Rail is a customer of Kopex.*
Above left: *1960s production.*
Below: *Kopex today.*

Recycling and remaining environment friendly

It is one of life's ironies that the vast amount of paperwork that comes through from the Government and its agencies might be dropping on the desk at the offices of WN Thomas and Son. This is one of the best places for it to arrive. Better still, if the bumph were written on metal. The Thomas company could deal with that, too. Since 1850, when William Thomas established his waste recovery business, the family firm has been dealing with the collection and recycling of waste materials. These days, the volume of material coming out from the Environment Agency and the EEC regulators at Brussels has to be taken seriously. Particularly since 1990, the whole industry has been swamped with masses of regulations and new working practices foisted upon it. However, it was a case of needs must and sink or swim. WN Thomas and Son recognised its responsibility, both to its own future and in its duty to the environment. Sleeves were rolled up and the challenge taken head on. By 1993 it had become the first scrap yard to become fully

licensed in the south east. This is an achievement in which it takes great pride. To help deal more fully with the safe and efficient disposal needs of today's engineering and manufacturing firms, a waste transfer station was opened on the premises in 1998. All types of waste could now be accepted. The firm's expertise and high standing in its field was recognised the same year by the Thames Valley Business Enterprise Award.

Although a limited company, the business has kept that family feel to it that has served the area for 150 years. All of the directors are family members and the staff are

Right: *A works outing, 1910.*
Below: *The winning turnout from the Royal Counties Agricultural Society Show in 1899.*

Wokingham. It had moved through the horse and cart era to a time of the lorry clanking along its path to Slough. By 1970, this was a business with a turnover running into seven figures. There was a large fleet of lorries, cranes, forklift trucks, a weighbridge, balers, power shears and every other piece of machinery imaginable. Offices had been opened in Stoke Gardens and the future was assured.

Over the last 30 years of the 20th century, the client base continued to grow.

regarded as part of that extended family. They are included on outings and the company offers an efficient and friendly service to its customers. The founder would have approved of the way the business has grown. He began in a small way in Wokingham, Berkshire. After some 20 years there, business transferred to Windsor. During the first world war, the collection and recycling of metal became more than just a business; it became part of the nation's survival. Railings, sheds, pots and pans were all put into 'the melting pot' to help provide more guns and shell casings for the war effort. Some of the tanks that rolled their way through the Battle of Cambrai owed their existence to the scrap metal merchant and the householder. The same appeals would be made in the 1940s. After the Great War, WN Thomas extended its influence by opening another centre in Slough.

In 1932, tragedy hit the family with the death of William Nosworthy Thomas Jr. The huge responsibility of running a growing and vibrant company fell upon his son, JR (Pat) Thomas. This was an awesome task for anyone. As Pat was only 20 years old at the time, it could have proved too much for one of such tender years. That it was anything but can be measured by the state of the company today. He took over what had been begun by his great grandfather. Once it had been a man with a barrow, touring the highways and byways around

People knew that a first class service was guaranteed. The skip collection service has been expanded and there is a balance in the business between the needs of industry and the householder. Even though it deals with giants like ICI and Lucas, the 'little man' has not been forgotten. Nickel, chrome, tungsten, steel and more keep the Thomas yards busy. Recycling scrap metal is vital in protecting the environment and safeguarding raw materials for our economic future. WN Thomas and Son Ltd has the experience and expertise.

Top left: 1960 metal shearing machine.
Top right: J R Thomas.
Below: New fleet of lorries arrived 1958.

Putting the zip into British Industry

Really good inventions have a way of being quickly taken for granted, then improved upon, then developed in new directions that the original inventor never even dreamed of. So it was with the telephone, the computer . . . even the zip fastener.

The invisible or concealed zipper was developed during the 1950s. Prior to that the only zippers had been the conventional, metallic chain ones, but when a certain Mr Mulka, of Paderborn, registered his design of a zipper with both outer and inner elements, he found a ready market for his invention. The world rights were acquired by Swiss-registered company SECO. However, SECO did not have the machinery to manufacture the zipper, and in 1952 it approached Mr B Bercovitz, the owner of engineering and trading companies in the USA, Canada and Europe, offering him an opportunity to purchase the rights and suggesting that the design and development work could be undertaken at a small plant near Zurich. Mr Bercovitz had a feasibility report prepared by Dr Doelter, and the following year preliminary work on the project began - not, as SECO had hoped, in Switzerland, but at Mr Bercovitz's Self Priming Pump and Engineering Limited (SPE Ltd) factory, in Slough.

The first machine parts were duly made in the Slough factory and assembled in a tiny basement workshop in London, and on 3rd October 1953 the first short length of Mulka zipper was produced. It consisted of plain cotton tape and aluminium elements, and the slider body bore the letters 'SPE'. By December of that year the complete Mulka textile zipper was being produced on the experimental prototype machines made by Dr Doelter and his team.

Top left: *Mr Mulka (inventor).*
Right: *Protective cover for missile warhead.*

The New Zipper Company was then established as a separate entity from SPE Limited, and during the years which followed the new company concentrated on meeting the various challenges inherent in launching a brand-new product onto the market. There was machinery to be developed; new manufacturing techniques to be devised; there was the question of the best material to use; work had to be carried out to improve the breaking strength of the zipper and the overall quality of the product. Then the economics of the whole project had to be assessed, and here facts came to light that gave rise to some concern; it seemed that the manufacturing costs of the concealed zipper would be so high that the product would have to be sold at almost three times the cost of a conventional zipper. However, as work progressed, experiments with impregnated cotton tape, which it was thought could be used in water-repellent zippers for raincoats, had raised the possibility of producing the world's only completely waterproof zipper. Such a product could command a far higher price, and so more work was carried out

Meanwhile the NZCo had moved into new, larger premises in Perth Avenue on the Slough Trading Estate, where by the summer of 1954 some 16 people were employed. Here the machines and other equipment were built, while the drawing office remained in London. Early the following year much larger premises in Berwick Avenue were acquired, and for the first time the whole team was brought together on the same site.

With the product perfected, all that remained was to develop its applications and markets. In addition to the obvious use in diving suits, applications for the BDM zipper (so called after financier Bercovitz, engineer Doelter and inventor Mulka) over the

in this direction. Various materials and rubber proofings were tried out for the tapes, including the new synthetic rubber Neoprene which gave very good results; and in August 1955 the company's wisdom in pursuing this particular direction was confirmed when the Ministry of Supply in London awarded it a development contract. Work went on; hurdles were overcome one by one; and eventually the company had a reliable, highly marketable and unique range of light, air, gas, water and chemical-proof total barrier zippers - something which the US manufacturers had been trying to achieve for 20 years, without success.

years have included submarine escape suits, high altitude flying suits, protective clothing, protective covers for expensive equipment (including Rolls-Royce aero engines) likely to be stored for considerable periods, airtight and watertight covers for Pye mobile radio phones, and rocket fuel handlers' suits. Its zippers have found uses all over the world - and its furthest-travelled zippers of all time were the ones in the spacesuits used in NASA's Mercury, Gemini and Apollo flight programmes!

Top: *New Zipper Company staff pictured in 1985.*
Above: *RAF Air and Ground crew wear uniforms fitted with New Zipper Company fastenings.*

Distributing innovation, expertise and excellence

S EI Macro, founded in 1969 as Macro-Marketing Ltd, has grown into one of those rare organisations that somehow contrive to be all things to all people. To the electronics industry, the SEI Macro Group is one of the foremost component distribution companies. The world's business community correctly perceives it as an expanding broadline distribution company, established across the UK and Ireland and with a strong market presence in the Eastern European sector. To its thousands of customers, SEI Macro means value-added support services, reliable delivery and innovative cost-reducing ideas; while to employees SEI Macro offers a dynamic, stimulating and supportive working environment where the emphasis is very much on teamwork.

Thirty years ago Macro was just as enthusiastic but much smaller; for the ten years which preceded the arrival of its first computer, the team performed wonders with manual stock record cards and electric typewriters, in a former hardware shop in the Bath Road. Company folklore recalls that the shocking pink net curtains which adorned Macro's front windows made the place look so much like a beauty salon from the outside that ladies regularly popped in to make an appointment for a perm or a purple rinse.

The embryonic electronics industry which Macro had been created to serve grew rapidly, and Macro grew with it. It bought the bungalow next door, the plumbing workshop, and the old shop stores, then it bought the garden and built on it, before eventually moving out to Burnham Lane into what used to be the local bowling alley.

From the beginning, Macro established itself as a specialist distributor, and a pioneer in its field. Focusing exclusively on semiconductor technology, it took on the Fairchild franchise, and subsequently that of Texas Instruments (for whom one of its founders, Rod Michell,

Right: *Macro's offices in the Bath Road, Slough in the 1970s.*

had previously worked). With financial backing from Diploma, the firm went on to acquire more and more franchise appointments from the leading manufacturers, and Macro became recognised by customers and suppliers alike as the largest, most successful and most efficient specialist service-led distribution company.

By the time of its silver jubilee, which it celebrated in August 1994, Macro was at the forefront of a very competitive semiconductor distribution industry and was branching out into a new PC component sector. Gone were the days when one person would pick up the phone, work out a quote for a customer using manufacturers' price lists, take the order, write out an IOF, produce an invoice, pack the goods and even set off to deliver it by hand. Motivation was as high as ever, but now, benefiting from the investment of around £1 million in modern IT equipment and refurbished premises, and including programming as a value-added service, the staff were able to support customers even more efficiently. This was quickly followed by the opening of a new 30,000 sq ft Logistics Centre and state-of-the-art programming facility in Crewe, Cheshire.

A major management restructure took place in 1997 when Diploma plc and SEI (Sonepar Electronique International), the leading European distribution group, became partners in a strategic joint venture, making the Macro Group part of the world's fourth largest electronic component distribution alliance. The SEI Macro Group, employing 330 people and

those of the PC market in the UK and across western and eastern Europe, and to service the latter the SEI Macro Group has set up a separate trading entity; Flashpoint, based alongside the parent company in Slough, has a multilingual 'call centre' which provides a 'one-stop shop' for system builders, and is one of the fastest growing specialist distributors of PC components.

The Group's early commitment to EDI (electronic data interchange) recently resulted in the company becoming the first electronic component distributor to win the coveted Award for Excellence in EDI; in this as in so many other

with an annual turnover in excess of £120 million, is one of the few distributors to have bridged the gap between global and local independent distributor. It is able to provide a truly local service, tailored to the demands of the customers in the market it serves; holding a comprehensive list of prestigious franchise agreements with the world's leading component manufacturers - currently numbering 68 and including such names as Sharp, Motorola, Hitachi, Texas Instruments, Siemens, Hewlett-Packard, ATI, Hyundai and Sony - the Group can offer its customers an impressive choice, combined with an unrivalled level of service, in both sectors of the market. The requirements of the industrial markets of the UK, Ireland and eastern Europe differ from

specialised fields, clients find SEI Macro's 'hands on' assistance invaluable, no matter how innovative and specialised their project may be. With a culture of innovation compounded by 30 years' practice of staying ahead in a fast-moving business, SEI Macro has acquired a blend of commercial and technological expertise which makes it uniquely capable of fulfilling the mission it has set for itself - excellence in customer service to the world.

Top: *The Order Processing Department at Bath Road in 1975. (The boxes on the desks are 'stock record cards'.)* ***Above:*** *The telesales floor at Macro, Burnham Lane in the 1980s.*

Mr Bunce, a CWS milkman in a picture dating from 1933. Handcarts were pulled around the street in the first home deliveries, but the horse drawn carts soon replaced these.

Acknowledgments

Slough Museum

Greville Creative Group

Slough Observer

Slough Express

Jane Bird

Thanks are also due to:
Andrew Mitchell who penned the editorial text and
Margaret Wakefield for her copywriting skills